# EU've got mail!

## Liberal Letters from the European Parliament
## by Graham Watson MEP

*Compiled and edited by Sarah Kent*

Published by Bagehot Publishing

The cover photo shows Graham Watson MEP voting in the
European Parliament's hemicycle

EU've got mail!
Liberal Letters from the European Parliament
by Graham Watson MEP
Compiled and edited by Sarah Kent

ISBN 0-9545745-1-6

Photos: PA Photos Ltd (Cover)
Philippe Lermusiaux
Thierry Monasse

Published in June 2004 by:
Bagehot Publishing
Bagehot's Foundry
Beard's Yard
Langport
Somerset TA10 9PS

Printed by:
Contract Printing
1 St James Road
St James Industrial Estate
Corby
Northants NN18 8AL


Publications by Graham Watson:

The Liberals in the North-South Dialogue (Ed.)
FNS, Bonn 1980

To the Power of Ten - essays from the European Parliament (Ed.)
CfR, London 2000

2020 Vision - Liberalism & Globalisation (Ed.)
CfR, London 2001

Liberal Language - speeches & essays 1998-2003
Bagehot Publishing, 2003

# Contents

## Introduction 4
*About Graham Watson* 8
*About the editor* 9

## Newsletters 2002 10

## Newsletters 2003 47

## Newsletters 2004 117

## Appendix of speeches 154
*Stability & Growth Pact (i) and enlargement (ii)* 154
*Liberal Democrat Autumn Conference, Brighton 2003* 158
*ELDR Congress, Amsterdam 2003* 165
*Italian Presidency of the EU* 173

*Index* 176
*Information/Addresses* 181

## Introduction

This book is a compilation of the weekly email newsletters I have written to Liberal Democrat party members in my constituency since shortly after my election in January 2002 as leader of the European Liberal Democrat and Reform party in the European Parliament. Ever keen to find new ways of communicating what I perceive to be happening in the EU (as opposed to what most of the UK's newspapers and too many of its broadcasters report), I decided to use the weekly commuting trips back to my constituency to record events and my opinion of them. The journey is normally a one hour aeroplane journey on Thursday evening from Brussels to Bristol. While other business travellers sleep, I tap away at a foldable keyboard which attaches to a palm-top computer. Arriving home in Langport some time after 2200 hrs I upload the text onto my home computer and email it to my office for distribution the following day to the mailing list of some 600 or so interested Liberal Democrats.

To my great pleasure and surprise it has proven a way to permit and encourage dialogue with party members who I may not otherwise see very often. Every week, between ten and twenty of those copied reply with views or information of their own or with requests for further information. This not only gives me a way of 'taking the temperature' on certain issues; it also provides me with instant feedback on my activity in the European Parliament.

Sadly, not all of the weekly emails have survived. I had not originally intended to collate and publish them and so did not take care to retain them. The first one or two are missing. Those for the weeks commencing 11 & 18 March 2002, 22 & 29 April 2002, 06 & 13 May 2002, 17 & 24 June 2002, 30 September 2002, 14 October 2002 and 22 November 2002 can also no longer be traced.

Re-reading the newsletters I have written over thirty months I note they have become longer and more detailed. This is in part a reflection of my growing understanding of the mechanics of EU government since my election to lead my colleagues. I know from readers' responses that many of them too have found the newsletters increasingly useful and I will endeavour to continue to write them as long as I remain in post.

The perspective of leadership is a challenging one. I rarely enjoy the luxury of spending a full week in Brussels or Strasbourg, our main places of work. Hardly a week goes by in which my presence is not required in one or other member state to rally the troops in our member parties. This work beyond Brussels is rendered considerably easier by the support of Germany's Friedrich Naumann Foundation. The professional advice and practical assistance willingly offered by their staff in central and eastern Europe and in Asia has been invaluable to me. The spread of Liberalism across the world owes much to their work.

Moreover, as Leader of my political group I do not sit on a committee. I am therefore prone to miss the first-hand knowledge and blow-by-blow understanding of how policies evolve. At the same time I am privileged to have access to meetings at which information is available to me which is not necessarily available to others. I also benefit hugely from the professional advice of the many able administrative staff employed by the ELDR Group.

One of my roles as parliamentary leader is to work together with the President of the ELDR party - during this period German Free Democrat MP Werner Hoyer - to convene meetings of the European Liberal Democrat Prime Ministers and Party Leaders from the EU and its candidate members on the eve of each EU summit. At the time of writing, we boast six prime ministers (Belgium, Denmark, Finland, Slovenia, Bulgaria and Turkey) plus the Presidents of the European Parliament and the European Commission. It is an impressive line up.

I believe there is potential benefit in extending this co-ordination to sectoral Councils. With Liberal Democrats represented in around half of the 25 member state governments, an awareness of ideological community could profitably be developed. The EU is not a confederation, but neither is it yet a federation. My aim is to encourage development towards federation.

My favourite sport is sailing. Regular short breaks at the helm of a yacht (in sunny climes whenever possible) help me to sustain the energy levels needed to do my job. Its principles can be applied to political leadership. As long as the course has been plotted and the crew are well briefed, a light touch on the tiller to guide and amplify the forces of nature is generally all that is needed.

I have sought to use my leadership to promote dialogue among the EU's Liberal parties. I have initiated regular conferences in Brussels to which I invite our relevant spokesperson from each national parliament, to keep them abreast of what is going on at EU level and to give my MEP colleagues the benefit of how different ideas might be received in the member states. I have also started a fortnightly email service to Liberal Democrat members of national parliaments to keep them abreast of legislative developments in Brussels and Strasbourg. I am convinced that to overcome the so-called 'democratic deficit' we must first improve co-ordination between members of the same political family at different levels of government. I first learned this when serving as Head of the Private Office to former Liberal Party leader David Steel at a time (1983 to 1987) when growing Liberal strength at local government level was not always recognised by the party's MPs at Westminster. Current lack of sympathy between national parliaments and the European Parliament has similarly undesirable consequences.

I try to use these weekly emails to party members in my constituency to inform and educate about the mechanisms of democracy at EU level as well as to report on current developments. This seems to work best by the use of examples pertaining to the passage of legislation or to parliamentary debates with the Council or Commission. But these newsletters are also to some extent a personal diary. One danger with any such format is that they become personal, petty bourgeois and individualistic. If they stray too far down that path I trust my readers will let me know!

I attempt to cover a range of topics, selecting those which might be of most interest to Liberal Democrats. Enlargement of the European Union from 15 to 25 members naturally features strongly, as does the discussion surrounding plans for a new EU Constitution. But economic policy, foreign policy (or lack of it), environmental policy and civil rights are all the subject of considerable coverage here, while individual legislative or other developments are frequently mentioned. This book is not a compendium of what happened in the European Union - or even the European Parliament - between January 2002 and May 2004. Nevertheless I hope that, alongside other testimonies, it will afford the reader an insight into developments which might otherwise be left in the cold hands of oblivion.

Robert Louis Stevenson once wrote in a letter to a friend who always preferred a reminiscence to a glass of wine that he sought to leave as much as possible of his life in his friends' letter boxes. Though I could match neither R.L. Stevenson's intellect, creative writing ability or humour I suppose this is part of a desire on my part to do the same. I hope it may please.

Graham Watson
June 2004

## About Graham Watson

Graham Watson was born in March 1956 in Rothesay, Scotland, the son of a Royal Naval officer and a teacher. He was educated at The City of Bath Boys' School and at Heriot Watt University, Edinburgh, where he gained an honours degree in Modern Languages. He is a qualified interpreter who speaks four European languages.

From 1983 to 1987 he served as Head of the Private Office of the Rt.Hon. Sir David Steel MP, then Leader of the Liberal Party. He had previously been active politically as General Secretary of the Liberal International's youth movement, and was a founder of the European Communities' Youth Forum.

Before entering parliament Graham Watson worked for the Hong Kong & Shanghai Banking Corporation in their London and Hong Kong offices, encompassing a three-month stint with the European Bank for Reconstruction and Development. He maintains an active interest in the Far East and is an Adviser to the Asia Pacific Public Affairs Forum.

Graham Watson was the first British Liberal Democrat to be elected to the European Parliament, winning the Somerset & North Devon constituency with a majority of over 22,500. In June 1999 Graham was elected to represent the new enlarged South West of England constituency, which covers Bristol, Gloucestershire, Somerset, Dorset, Wiltshire, Devon and Cornwall.

From 1994 to 1999, Graham was a member of the Committee for Economic & Monetary Affairs and Industrial Policy and of the Budgets Committee. From July 1999 to 2002 he served as Chairman of the Committee on Citizens' Freedoms and Rights, Justice and Home Affairs.

On 15 January 2002 Graham Watson was elected Leader of the 53 strong group of Liberal Democrat members of the European Parliament.

Graham lives with his wife and two children in the small market town of Langport, Somerset.

## About the Editor

Sarah Kent was born in Aldershot, Hampshire and grew up in the South West where she attended St. Michael's School, Tawstock and Taunton School. She gained an honours degree in European Union Studies with French and Italian at Cardiff University. After graduating, Sarah became parliamentary assistant to Graham Watson in Brussels, before taking up a position as Assistant Press and Public Relations Officer for the European Liberal Democrat and Reform Group in the European Parliament. Sarah left the European Parliament in 2004 to take part in the European Masters Degree programme in Human Rights and Democratisation, based in Venice.

# 2002

*2002 was an important year for the European Union. Not only did the fifteen member states have to contend with divided opinion over the escalating situation in Iraq, but it was also the year in which the Union would make a final decision about its own enlargement. The EU leaders' summit in Copenhagen in December would close negotiations with the ten 'first-wave' applicant states from central and eastern Europe (Poland, Hungary, the Czech Republic, Slovakia, Slovenia, Latvia, Lithuania, Estonia, Malta and Cyprus) and pave the way for the Union to welcome them formally in May 2004.*

*2002 also marked the entry of the euro into general circulation. All Member States bar the UK, Denmark and Sweden introduced the new currency on 01 January.*

*In this year, the European Parliament set up a Temporary Committee to examine the issues around the outbreak of Foot and Mouth Disease in Europe and particularly in the UK in 2001. The Committee was to focus on how to prevent similar outbreaks in the future.*

*The Convention on the future of Europe began its work in 2002. The European Council decided at its summit in Belgium (Laeken) in December 2001 to establish this Convention to draft an EU constitution (and revision of the current EU Treaties) to be adopted during an intergovermental conference in 2004. The Convention was presided over by former French President Valéry Giscard d'Estaing, and comprised representatives from governments, national parliaments, the European Parliament, European Commission and various observers. Its inaugural meeting was on 28 February.*

*Countries holding the office of Presidency of the EU in 2002 were Spain and Denmark.*

*Graham Watson was elected Leader of the 53-strong European Liberal Democrat and Reform Group in the European Parliament on 15 January 2002. His predecessor, Irish Liberal Pat Cox, became the second Liberal President of the European Parliament since its first direct elections in 1979.*

**Friday 15 February**

This week is one of the 'white weeks' in the European Parliament, when MEPs have no formal parliamentary business to deal with. I spent Monday and Tuesday in Brussels getting my feet under the desk in my new leadership role. I took the opportunity the rest of the week to accept an invitation from the Asia-Europe Foundation (ASEF) to join them to celebrate their fifth anniversary at a set of meetings in Singapore.

ASEF is involved in cultural and people-to-people exchanges between Asia and Europe, and their first five years have been a great success. Their presence in the next five will be just as important. Isolationist policies are no longer viable in an ever shrinking world, especially when things like terrorist acts planned in the Middle East take place in America on the other side of the world. That is why, in my role as leader of the European Parliament's Liberal Democrats, I am campaigning for Europe to engage with the rest of the world in finding common solutions to global problems, leaving national governments to decide on issues which only impact on one country.

In the UK, any mention of Europe will bring up the subject of the euro within seconds. In the rest of Europe this is a 'dead issue'.

The 1st January came and went, and people from Cork to Crete are using the euro to buy their bread and milk without any problems - many don't even think about it. Even in Denmark and Sweden (who chose not to join the euro-zone in referendums), public opinion is now substantially in favour of the euro.

Instead on the continent, the issue being talked about is EU enlargement, and the prospect of a Union covering much of Eastern Europe. I fully support this move; including these countries will enable the union to exercise real power, where only a pan-European decision will do.

## Friday 22 February

A big 'thank-you' to all the members from the Bristol area who came to the Redcliff Theatre in Clifton on Monday night to support me in my debate about the euro against Nigel Farage MEP of the UK Independence Party. Highlights of the debate will be shown on BBC2 on Sunday lunchtime. We beat them resoundingly, exposing all the flaws in their arguments against Britain joining the euro and showing their rowdy supporters up for the xenophobes they are.

Thank you too to those who came out in Cheltenham on Tuesday morning to help me campaign against the Northern Distributor Road, in support of our local election candidates; and in Malmesbury on Tuesday afternoon in support of North Wiltshire District Council by-election candidate Ann Davis.

On Wednesday and Thursday I was back in Brussels where I continued my work on the EU's measure to tackle terrorism[1] in meetings with the European Policy Centre (a Brussels think-tank) and with the Chairman of the Justice Committee in the US Senate and I took forward the Liberal Democrat campaign against the use of EU funds for an environmentally damaging hydrological project in Spain.

Today (Friday) sees a series of meetings in the constituency including a meeting in Bournemouth with Dorset members of the CBI. I will also be talking to new Western Counties Regional Chair Shirley Holloway about how best to use our new full time campaigns officers who I am paying for jointly with the region's MPs, the Regional Party and the Federal Party's Campaigns and Elections Department.

---

[1] *In 2001, Graham authored an 'own-initiative' report on combating terrorism in the EU. The report was adopted by Parliament on 05 September, just six days before the attacks on New York and Washington. His initial report formed the basis of the EU's reponse to combating terrorism, including the establishment of a European Arrest Warrant.*

## Friday 01 March

This week saw a mini plenary session of the parliament in Brussels. The session gave me an opportunity to outline my political priorities for my time as leader of the Liberal Democrat group in parliament.

First, looking towards enlargement of the Union, this year is decision year for enlargement, and we must be in a position to decide which of the applicant states are ready for admission by the end of the year. This places a heavy burden on Spain, the current holders of the EU presidency, to make good progress if we are to close all the negotiations in time. The Liberal Democrats' emphasis will be on ensuring that the relevant criteria for entry are fully respected.

Second, the forthcoming Barcelona summit could be an important milestone in taking forward the Lisbon agenda[1] if the political will is there. The Liberal Democrats will measure the success of that summit against progress towards the adoption of key legislation, including the pensions directive, liberalisation of energy markets and the European patent. If we are to make a success of enlargement, we must show the applicant states that we too are capable of the economic reform that we rightly expect of them.

And finally, the Convention on the Future of Europe (which held its first meeting on Thursday) offers a great opportunity to reconnect the EU to its citizens by enhancing democracy and transparency and by placing our common European rights and values at the centre of a new constitutional settlement. I am optimistic that with prominent members such as Andrew Duff (LibDem MEP for Eastern England) representing the European Liberal Democrats, we can make a substantial and positive impact.

[1] *The EU's Lisbon agenda, so-called after the EU Leaders' summit in Lisbon in 2000, aims to make the European Union 'the most competitive and dynamic knowledge-based economy in the world by 2010.'*

**Saturday 9 March**

This weekend's Lib Dem Spring Conference is an ideal opportunity to look at the recent successes of the Liberal Democrats, who not only hold the balance of power in Brussels, but are also in power in many local authorities, the Welsh Assembly and the Scottish Parliament.

Last night, at the pre-conference rally, we had a number of speakers from authorities and assemblies where we hold power - a true celebration of Liberal Democracy in action.

For my part, I led on the success that we have had in the chamber in Brussels in recent months - not least the anti-terrorism legislation that I recently piloted through the house.

But for all these successes, there are those in other parties, and in ours, who would rather see us fail. The following is an excerpt from my speech last night:

"We challenge Iain Duncan Smith and his tin hat territorials to show how the world would be a safer place if the tribes of Europe were still apart. If freebooting is their overriding value - more important than concerted action on climate change, more important than pooling resources to curb HIV infection in Africa, more important than making common cause against the drugs trade - then humankind would pay a heavy price for their happiness.

"I also read in the public press that some of our own MPs are set to challenge Charles' championing of Europe. That's OK - we're a big enough party to embrace differing views. But let it be honest dissent, honestly debated, not some closet committee-corridor cabal. If these MPs exist, let them show their colours, let us eyeball their ideas and test their alternatives. Our concept of government is clear - local wherever possible, national where appropriate and international where necessary."

I do hope that you will join with me to ensure that we continue to succeed in government, at local, regional, national and international levels - this really is an exciting time to be a Liberal Democrat.

**Thursday 28 March**

After a week's holiday, I will be back in Brussels next week attending the European Liberal Democrats' Spring Conference.

A distinguished panel of speakers and guests will try to formulate answers to a number of key questions: Which EU policy towards the Mediterranean and Middle-Eastern regions? How can we promote multiculturalism in European society? What is the role of the EU in the defence of human rights?

Looking ahead to the expansion of the EU into Eastern Europe, we will also be considering the applications of various political parties to join the European Liberal Democrats - in particular we look forward to welcoming new member parties from the emerging democracies from Central & Eastern Europe. I have invested a lot of my own time in encouraging such applications, having visited Liberal parties in the Czech Republic, Bulgaria and Hungary over the past three weeks. The conference will also address the state of play with the new Convention on the Future of the EU.

The months ahead look to be a very exciting time for the Liberal Democrats in Europe, as the EU expands, and its true value in a shrinking world becomes apparent, and I am therefore very honoured to be leading our parliamentary group at the present moment.

**Saturday 06 April**

Yesterday morning it gave me great pleasure to accept two new member parties into the European Liberal Democrats. The new parties - the Free Citizens Movement from Greece and the Alliance for the New Citizen (ANO) from Slovakia (which is expected to be included in the next wave of countries joining the EU) add very much to the diversity and strength of our party in Europe. We already hold the balance of power in the European Parliament, but as the EU expands we need to make sure that we are firmly rooted in the new member states so as to build on the position we are in at the moment.

This strength and diversity is one of the reasons that I am so proud to be welcoming the European Liberal Democrats' Autumn Conference to Bath this year (a subject that was discussed at length in Brussels on Thursday evening). Another reason is the simple fact that the conference will bring over half a million pounds into the region. The conference is being held from 16 to 18 October in and around the Pump Rooms in the centre of Bath.

Today I've been reporting back on the past few months' work in the European Parliament to the Devon County Council Liberal Democrat Group at their away day in Exeter. There really has been a lot happening in Parliament, not least the setting up of a Foot and Mouth Inquiry, work on sustainable development, the approval of an Environment Action Programme and reform of the Common Agricultural Policy - all directly effecting Devon in some way. Indeed, on the subject of Foot and Mouth, I am pleased to be able to receive Nick Clegg MEP (LibDem, East Midlands) and Jan Mulder MEP (Liberal, Netherlands) in Devon towards the end of this month to show them the devastating effects of the disease on the county. Both of these MEPs sit on the Parliament's Foot and Mouth Inquiry.

There'll be more news about this visit in the coming weeks - along with more news about the Bath conference.

**Monday 15 April**

On Thursday the world moved one step closer to setting up a permanent International Criminal Court in The Hague. The court will pass judgement on the most grievous war crimes and crimes against humanity across the world, committed after it comes into being.

This court will have a key role to play. So far the only response to war crimes and crimes against humanity has been temporary and ad hoc tribunals set up after the event. In many of these cases the perpetrators believed that they would never face justice, but with a permanent court they will be in no doubt before they commit their crimes that justice will follow.

It is for this reason that I have been campaigning for an international court since I was first elected as an MEP in 1994. In 1998 the campaign succeeded and the UN laid down the foundations for the court in the Rome Treaty - but it could not come into force until half of the UN's members ratified the treaty. I am delighted that that day has finally come.

It is, however, disappointing that some fairly serious international players are missing. Russia, China and the United States have all failed to ratify the treaty, and the Bush administration is clear in its disagreement. This is a tragedy for international justice, and I will be joining the calls for the US to change its policy.

However, I am confident that justice will prevail, and that nations which are yet to embrace the court will soon become convinced that it is a force for good.

**Friday 24 May**

This past week was a committee week in Brussels, when all the various parliamentary committees held their meetings. The Fisheries Committee held a hearing during the week which heard evidence from Fisheries Commissioner, Franz Fischler and Neil Kinnock, the Administration Commissioner about the 'sacking' of the Director General for Fisheries, Steffan Smidt. This follows allegations that Spain had intervened improperly into EU policy by insisting in a telephone call from the Spanish Prime Minister Aznar to Head of the Commission, Romano Prodi that Smidt had to go because his concerns were upsetting Spanish fishermen.

The outcome of the hearing will be presented to the political group leaders who will decide whether a parliamentary inquiry is necessary.

Later in the week Romano Prodi presented the European Commission's proposal for the future structure of European government to the Convention on the Future of Europe. These proposals contained little which is surprising, but are an important restatement of the need to have a strong European Commission holding the ring to ensure fair play in the fight between the national interests of member states.

Liberal Democrats are broadly supportive of the proposals, which may lead to the eventual creation of an EU foreign minister as defence and security policies of the member states are brought together.

Next week, we meet again in plenary in Brussels, and in next week's email I will inform you of the latest developments there.

**Friday 31 May**

This week has seen a part-sitting[1] of the European Parliament in Brussels. There were two items of particular interest to the South West on the agenda, one about the reform of the Common Fisheries Policy, and the other about competition in car sales across Europe.

As we have known for years the present Common Fisheries Policy is seriously flawed, and at last the European Commission has accepted this. The CFP has caused hardship and uncertainty in our fishing industry, while failing miserably to achieve its aim of conserving fish stocks.

If fishing is to have a future, trawler capacity has to be reduced. With too many boats competing for too few fish it has been nonsense for the EU to allow Spain and France to use EU money to build new trawlers and I welcome the plan to scrap this scheme and instead do more to help fishermen to find new work. Fishermen and those who rely on jobs associated with fishing want a long-term stable industry with reasonable rewards.

What we now need is a commitment by the EU member states to approve the Commission's plan. The plan is based on scientific evidence and the member states must take proper account of the advice rather than indulge in the annual round of horse-trading to set quotas that goes on at the moment. Fishermen should be more involved and should be consulted more. Their views and knowledge should be taken into account.

It is also essential that enforcement of the rules should be seen to be equitable throughout the EU.

On Thursday morning there was a vote in Parliament on a report from the Economic Affairs Committee, recommending that the opening up of the car sales market in Europe be delayed until 2005.

At present the car industry is exempt from normal European competition rules under what is known as a block exemption agreement. The problem with this is that the car industry can continue making it difficult for UK nationals to buy cars on the continent and bring them back to the UK. And of course, the result of this is that we in the UK pay far more for our new cars than almost anyone in the rest of the EU.

I and my Liberal Democrat colleagues voted against the recommendation to delay the opening of the market, but we were defeated. However, when this subject comes up again, I will continue my fight for the sensible opening of competition in this vital market.

Finally, make I take this opportunity to wish you a very peaceful Jubilee holiday weekend.

[1] *The European Parliament's official seat is in Strasbourg, France, where MEPs hold their plenary sessions for a week every month. Pressure of work has led to a further six two-day sessions being held eveyr year in Brussels. All sessions are known officially as 'part sittings'.*

## Friday 07 June

While those of you in the UK had two bank holidays at the beginning of the week, it has been a normal 5 day week in Brussels - and a busy one at that, with a lot of meetings as leader of the Liberal Democrat group in the Parliament.

*EU've got mail!*

The biggest question facing the rest of the EU at the moment isn't the euro, that's old news on the continent now - but the expansion of the EU into Eastern Europe. On Monday I met with senior Commission officials and a Polish Government minister to discuss just this subject, and the economic benefits that it will bring to countries like Poland.

And on Thursday I hosted a reception to launch Will Hutton's new book 'The World We're In' in which he discusses how events like September 11 and globalisation in general affect the Union in Europe. Later on I hosted a co-ordination dinner for the Liberal Democrat members of the Convention on the Future of Europe, which include Lord (Bob) Maclennan[1] as a UK representative on the Convention. The Convention is currently discussing what changes need to be made to the institutions of the EU in the light of its enlargement, and is due to report at the end of the year.

As ever, as well as looking at enlargement, I have had a number of meetings with Liberal Democrats in countries within the EU. I was in Copenhagen on Tuesday meeting Danish Government ministers - Denmark takes over the presidency of the EU on 01 July, and has a Liberal government. We'll then see Liberal Democrats at the head of all the major institutions in the EU - the Parliament, Commission, and Council Presidency - a great success that can only help in the spreading of our policy and beliefs.

Next week we are back in Strasbourg where Parliament will sit in plenary session for the week.

[1] *Lord Maclennan of Rogart is a Liberal Democrat peer, and the LibDem spokeperson in the Lords on Europe.*

### Friday 14 June

All the fuss about immigration this week[1] is designed to counter a tendency of voters in some countries to vote for the extreme right. It is pure PR spin. Why? Because EU governments all recognise first that the EU needs about one million immigrants a year to satisfy the needs of the labour market (due to our ageing populations); and second that they have to work together if they are to have any control whatsoever over immigration. The 'zero-immigration' policies that they have tried have failed, and they know that in order effectively to shut the back door of illegal immigration they will need to open the front door a little with a legal immigration policy.

Justice and Home Affairs ministers might have agreed this last year but their attention was distracted by the need for tougher anti- terrorism laws after September 11. Chances are they will reach agreement by the end of this year once they stop posturing and get down to business.

Good news for pedestrians this week. Liberal Democrats in the European Parliament brokered an agreement with the car industry to stop putting 'bull-bars' on vehicles or selling them as additional parts. The ban comes into effect immediately and will be followed with legislation to improve other aspects of car design to reduce pedestrian injuries in accidents.

Finally, the Torquay Express & Herald from Devon and the Stroud News from Gloucestershire had journalists in Strasbourg this week at my invitation. They witnessed the 'Reuniting Europe' event at which I hosted 23 'virtual MEPs', in reality national MPs from the Eastern European candidate countries due to join the EU in 2004. Liberal Democrats are trying to raise the profile of the debate on EU enlargement to make sure our short-sighted national governments do not allow short-term concerns to derail the process of uniting the two halves of our continent.

[1] *UK Prime Minister Tony Blair and Spanish Premier José Maria Aznar had billed the coming EU Leaders' summit in Seville as one which would get tough on illegal immigration. The issue had shot to the top of the summit agenda following the strength of far-right parties in French and Dutch elections.*

## Friday 05 July

This week the importance of the Liberal Democrats in the European Parliament as the party that holds the balance of power was shown once again.

On Wednesday we narrowly voted to toughen draft proposals from the Commission on the labelling and tracing of GM ingredients through the food-chain. With the two major socialist (Labour) and centre right (Conservative) political groups supporting opposite sides of the argument, it was thanks to the Liberal group that the proposals were passed.

We voted that the threshold for food containing GM material that has to be labelled is 0.5% (or lower if scientifically possible), rather than the 1% threshold proposed by the Commission. We also voted for the labelling of animal feed bought by farmers containing GM ingredients, and the labelling of products containing GM ingredients even if they are not scientifically detectable, but are identified only through paper-chase traceability schemes.

I am particularly pleased that we have voted through a sensible package of measures which will give consumers maximum information about the food they are going to eat, but one that does not put non-GM food producers at a disadvantage by obliging them to label their products as GM-free. This will allow consumers to make up their own minds without being given so much information that shopping trips become a nightmare.

You may remember a few weeks ago that I mentioned that the International Criminal Court, an institution that I have consistently campaigned for since first being elected in 1994, had been given the go-ahead. It is most unfortunate to hear this week that the USA, who have not yet signed up to the court, are trying negotiate immunity for their troops, and if they don't get their way they are threatening to withdraw their troops from UN missions around the globe.

It is vital that this Court is a success. Only then will the perpetrators of serious war crimes who at present think that they will not face justice think twice before committing their crimes. The stance taken by the USA is most unhelpful, and can only lead to the undermining of international justice. I will therefore be lobbying the US Government hard during my visit to Washington DC next week to discuss EU / US relations.

**Friday 12 July**

The European Parliament went into recess this week and I have been in North America for meetings with officials in Washington DC and in Ottawa.

In the United States I met officials from the White House, the State Department and the fledgling Department for Homeland Security to talk about how Europe can best help America fight terrorism (I piloted the package of anti-terrorism measures through the European Parliament last autumn while I was chairman of Parliament's Committee on Justice and Home Affairs). I told them of Europe's concern that the USA is isolating itself by its refusal to sign the Kyoto Convention on climate change, the UN Convention on the Rights of the Child and the Ottawa Land Mines Convention and trying to undermine the new International Criminal Court. I was pleased to discover over supper with Madeleine Albright, former US Ambassador to the UN and leading member of the Clinton Administration, that the Democratic Party shares our concerns.

In Ottawa I expressed support for Canada's helpful participation in all the international conventions mentioned above and discussed with officials how Canada and Europe can put pressure on the US to revoke their recently imposed steel tariffs (which led to the closure of a steel works in Wales this week) and their protectionist farm subsidies which threaten to undermine work in the World Trade Organisation to help developing countries. I also spoke to Liberal Party officials and MPs about the damaging leadership contest which is currently dividing Canada's Liberal Party, the most successful Liberal Party in government over many years.

On arrival at Heathrow on Friday morning I drove to Exeter to attend the South West Regional Assembly, which was discussing the Government's plans to allow regional government in England and the new proposals for transport policy in the region. I attend many of these meetings, to which MPs and MEPs are invited to report, and I am full of admiration for the work of our Liberal Democrat colleagues who sit on the assembly, and provide the driving force of its politics.

The European Parliament will be in recess until Monday 26 August. I will spend next week visiting constituents in Cornwall and the following week clearing up odds and ends in Brussels before taking a holiday with my family.

**Friday 30 August**

Bank Holiday Monday found MEPs back at their desks in Brussels. Unlike Westminster, our summer break runs from late July to late August; and the Brussels timetable pays no respect to individual national holidays. The last week of August involves meetings of the political parties here, so I found myself chairing a discussion by 52 suntanned Liberal Democrat MEPs of next week's plenary session agenda in Strasbourg.

The two most important items on next week's agenda are both issues on which the ELDR Group has provided the "rapporteur", the person appointed to pilot the legislation through its committee stages. My Dutch colleague Marieke Sanders has brought forward the proposal to create what is known as 'a single European sky', which will stop French (or any other) air traffic controllers making European holidaymakers' lives a misery. And a Belgian Liberal Democrat, Ward Beysen, is presenting Parliament's response to European Commission proposals to harmonise laws on sales promotions, so that a company making a 'buy one get one free' offer can do so across the EU without being held up by restrictive German regulations which outlaw them.

At the level of grand-standing politics, Liberal Democrats in the EP will be leading the calls for a debate on the U.S. proposals for military action against Iraq. The Socialists prefer to debate the floods in Germany and the Czech Republic, because their powerful German component thinks it could help their chances in the German general election this month, and the right wing is divided over whether to support George Bush. Nonetheless we may win the day, since the issue is so important.

We will strike a blow for freedom too in a report by another Dutch colleague, Jules Maaten, whose report on the EU's relations with Asia calls for the first time for the inclusion of Taiwan in the regular Asia-Europe co-operation talks.

But before then I've another weekend's round of constituency engagements, including a preview of the new British and Commonwealth museum in Bristol. A better knowledge of our heritage may help me to understand why the UK is sometimes so reluctant to embrace European co-operation. For me, using our electronic voting cards in the European Parliament to resolve our differences is preferable to throwing hand grenades at each other across the western front.

**Sunday 08 September**

Fortunately the Alsatian sun shone for Parliament's first autumn session this week. Strasbourg is resplendent in the sunshine, with Parliament's award-winning building reflected peacefully in the canal and its neighbour the European Court of Human Rights gracing the more turbulent waters along the nearby riverbank. Not that I had much time to stand and stare! I had to be there for 9am Monday for a meeting of the executive committee of the ELDR Party (which meant leaving the UK on Sunday afternoon), which put the finishing touches to the programme for the ELDR's annual conference, to be held from 16 to 18 October in Bath, the only world heritage city in my constituency.

The Liberal Democrat (ELDR) group met on Monday afternoon and agreed our amendments to the 17 reports on this week's order paper. We are fortunate to have a higher turnout of our members at votes and a higher cohesion rate (ie we all vote the same way), than the other political groups, which meant that this week we could secure the passage of the Regulation on Sales Promotions, eliminating some of the remaining barriers to trade among the EU countries.

On Tuesday I met other MEPs to discuss a campaign to limit the concentration of media power in too few hands, which is a danger to pluralism in the UK (Rupert Murdoch), Italy (Silvio Berlusconi), Germany (Bestelsman/Kirsch) and Luxembourg (RTL). We hope to secure a statement and a debate next month.

Iraq was the subject of our first debate on Wednesday; I urged caution. If the Americans strike without international backing or plans for rebuilding the country afterwards I fear an implosion in the region which would increase the danger. I fear George W Bush wants to settle an old family score with Saddam Hussein; conveniently it would take public attention away from the USA's failure to capture Osama bin Laden.

On Thursday I came home early. There was nothing hugely important on our agenda and since it was my 15th wedding anniversary I wanted to take Rita out for an evening to ourselves.

## Friday 13 September

Inflammation of the sciatic nerve (between vertebrae L4 and L5 for the cognoscenti among my readers) has dogged me since last weekend, making this week the most unpleasant in my eight years in the European Parliament. When your diary fills up ten to twelve weeks in advance, however, there's little you can do but soldier on, which meant travelling to Riga in Latvia on Monday morning to lecture to university students about the EU, then meet Prime Minister Andris Berzins (a Liberal Democrat) and other leading party figures to try and boost their flagging general election campaign (they go to the polls on 5 October). In a country which has only half the population of my constituency, a visit from the leader of a political party in the European Parliament attracts a lot of media interest. I hope it helps our Liberal Democrat friends there.

Latvia's plans to join the EU, which I discussed with Prime Minister Berzins, are progressing well. With any luck they will be among the countries which we agree to admit to the Union in 2004. They hope to join NATO at the same time. Decisions will be made at the NATO summit in Prague in November and at the EU summit in Copenhagen in December.

Back in Brussels on Wednesday the European Parliament held a special ceremony in commemoration for the victims of last year's terrorist attacks on the USA. In my speech I sought to move the debate on, urging EU governments to review the anti-terrorist legislation which we put in place in a hurry last year. Unless they do this we risk being passed by the Americans into putting further measures in place which, in my view, would threaten important civil liberties such as personal privacy and the right of a defendant to a fair trial.

On Thursday I met Pavel Rusko, the leader of Slovakia's Liberal Democrats. They too have elections shortly (22 September) and I had arranged a programme of meetings for him with bigwigs in Brussels to help his campaign. He came well prepared with two Slovak TV crews at his heels.

Later I received constituents John Ruane and Christine Lee of Cheltenham. They run a non-governmental organisation called 'Naturewatch' and were in Brussels to promote animal welfare issues. It's good to see that my constituency spawns organisations like this.

This afternoon I drive to Stroud to speak at our Lib Dem Constituency supper in their Liberal Club. The doctor told me to cut down on travelling because of my back, but this supper had been arranged for weeks and well advertised locally and I do not want to let them down.

**Saturday 21 September**

The highlight of my week has been the success in bringing to my constituency Commissioner Michel Barnier and Luciano Caveri MEP,

*EU've got mail!*

who are respectively the European Commissioner and the European Parliament Committee Chair responsible for regional policy and the EU structural funds. I left Brussels early on Thursday lunchtime, to fly with the regional policy committee chair to Bristol, where we looked at inner-city regeneration projects funded by the EU. Then we drove to Devon to meet councillors and officials involved in running Objective 2 programmes there, including our own Councillor Des Shadrick of Devon County Council. On Friday morning Commissioner Barnier joined us for a conference in Plymouth on how Objective 1 works for Cornwall. In my experience, bringing the decision makers to see for themselves often helps secure more money in the future. At least, that's what I'm aiming for.

I'd flown to Brussels from Bristol on the 'red-eye-express' on Monday morning with student Douglas Benedict of Salisbury, who joined me for a week's work experience. He came with me to most of the various meetings and conferences which fill a party leader's week, though on Tuesday he work shadowed Sarah Kent (a former work experience trainee herself from Somerset) in my press office while I flew to London to meet Europe Minister Peter Hain MP and to speak at a Federal Trust conference. I used the occasion to highlight one of our Liberal Democrat proposals to the Convention on the Future of Europe, namely to write into the new EU treaty a clause allowing a member state to decide to quit the EU. Though the USA has no secession clause in its constitution, I believe that the EU should have. That way we might avoid the bloody civil war fought in the USA when South Carolina wanted to leave.

Wednesday and Thursday morning were spent chairing meetings of the Liberal MEPs to discuss the agenda for next week's plenary session in Strasbourg. On Thursday morning I invited Neil Kinnock, Commissioner for Administration and Reform, to come to our meeting and defend himself against allegations by an official, Marta Andreasen, that the EU's accounting practices are a shambles. Her accusations have excited a lot of interest in the UK, where Tory euro-sceptics have pounced on them, but nowhere else. Why? Because Mrs Andreasen was suspended from a job at the OECD (Organisation for Economic Co-operation and Development) two years ago for the same reason:

recruited to help in reforming the accounts, but not up to the job, she turned the tables on her colleagues in a welter of recrimination. I am convinced that Kinnock is doing a good job in carrying out the reforms urged by the EU's Court of Auditors. But, as he freely admits, overhauling the public accounts is a big job and while it's underway, the critics, like the devil, have the best tunes.

**Sunday 29 September**

This week was a Strasbourg week, when Parliament meets in plenary session for our formal debates and votes. For me however, the week started on Sunday with the Liberal Democrat Party Conference in Brighton where Charles Kennedy gathered MPs, MEPs and members of the Scottish and Welsh Parliaments together for a meeting and photocall. I was able to stay at conference only until 5pm on Monday, but managed to fit in meetings with many visitors and delegates and a speech to a fringe meeting about regional government in England. I am a founder member of the South West Constitutional Convention and I told the delegates how I hoped the South West would be among the first regions to have a directly elected assembly.

While many of my MEP colleagues decided to stay in Brighton, I had no choice, as Leader of the 53 Liberal Democrat MEPs but to 'hot foot' it to Strasbourg.

On Tuesday I convened a meeting of MEPs to discuss the damage to democracy posed by powerful media monopolies in Britain, Germany and Italy. I was able to secure agreement that we will debate this issue with the European Commission in November.

On Wednesday I led for the Liberal Group in the debate on the permanent International Criminal Court. I criticised European governments for failing to take a firm stand against the USA, which wants to give its own soldiers immunity from prosecution for crimes committed in war. To my mind, the International Criminal Court (which starts operations next January) should have the power to prosecute anybody guilty of crimes against humanity.

Parliamentary business has kept me in Strasbourg late into the week. We have a very heavy workload at present, with major decisions to be taken on the reform of the Common Agricultural Policy and bringing up to 10 new countries into the European Union.

Nonetheless, I found time to have supper with Lord Russell Johnston, former MP for Inverness and one of my mentors in politics.

**Friday 11 October**

The main European Parliament news of this week was the publication of the progress report on candidate countries. The Commission's "best guess", since enlargement of the EU is still 18 months away, is that ten new countries will be ready to join us in 2004. There are still problems to be overcome: border controls need to be improved, more done to fight corruption, economies to be further freed of the heavy hand of Soviet-style state control. But Poland, Hungary, the Czech Republic, Slovakia, Slovenia, the Baltics, Malta and Cyprus will - if our fifteen Heads of State and Government agree to it in Copenhagen in December - soon join us. In my speech on behalf of the Liberal Democrat group I argued for continued monitoring, both of applicant countries and existing Member States, to see that democratic and free-market standards are maintained. I pointed out that 18 months before Britain joined the EEC in 1973 we were still struggling to meet the entry criteria; and I added flippantly that some say we're still struggling 30 years later! Liberal Democrats right across Europe have supported early EU entry for the newly liberated countries of central and eastern Europe. Better to stabilise their freedoms by anchoring them in the Union than to pay the price of cleaning up ancient ethnic hatreds later on, as we had to in the former Yugoslavia.

Other highlights of the week were visits to Parliament by 35 Libdem members from the Yeovil and Taunton constituencies, organised by Hilary Leaman; and a visit from Charles Kennedy on Thursday. Charles visited NATO, spoke to the British Chamber of Commerce and held talks with UK Lib Dem MEPs. We told him it's not only in the UK that the Party is being taken more seriously nowadays: across Europe, Liberal Democrat parties are increasingly successful.

Parliament voted on Thursday on emissions trading, deep-sea fisheries and a new association agreement with Algeria. On the latter, Liberal Democrats led the campaign to insist on better protection for human rights before the Algerian government gets further EU support. Current abuses are among the worst in Africa. We won the votes!

Now for a very full weekend of constituency campaigning, including unusually a commitment on a Sunday - but it's in Weymouth, so perhaps we'll take the children to the beach at the same time.

**Friday 25 October**

As I write, Europe's national presidents and prime ministers are gathering in Brussels for a summit meeting to thrash out the financial details of bringing ten new member countries into the EU. They agreed the overall budget two years ago in Berlin. What they now have to decide is how much of the total will be spent on direct income support to farmers in the new countries, how much on the structural funds (Objective 1 and so on) and how much on budget compensation. (Budget compensation means money that will be paid directly to these countries if they find they are net contributors before 2006, i.e. if the money they pay in in VAT and excise duties is greater than what they recive from the CAP and the structural funds.)

The deal on offer to the new countries is, frankly, ungenerous. As Janesz Drnovsek, the Slovenian Prime Minister (a Lib Dem) pointed out at our Liberal family leaders' lunch today, Slovenia will be competing with Ireland, Portugal and Greece yet receiving only a quarter as much from the CAP and less than half as much from the structural funds. Nonetheless they would be a net payer whereas those three existing members are all net beneficiaries!

Reform of the Common Agricultural Policy (i.e. cutting the amount spent) and the question of Britain's budget rebate are irrelevant to this week's debate, but they have been raised because France and Germany - who will have to pay a lot - want in return some guarantees about how the EU will be financed after 2006 when the Berlin financing agreement expires.

My fear is that an historic opportunity to unite a divided continent may slip away in a welter of recrimination as an unholy alliance of egoists and cowards (our national leaders) squabble over the bill. The current President of the Council of Ministers, Danish Liberal Democrat Anders Fogh Rasmussen, has worked hard to get a successful outcome but nothing is yet certain. If they fail to agree this week, the matter will have to await the Copenhagen summit in December, and any deal reached there would then have to be presented to the applicant country leaders on a take-it-or-leave-it basis. Our leaders need to show they are statesmen and not simply politicians.

Other big issues in Parliament this week (we were in plenary session in Strasbourg) were:

- a debate with Commission President Romano Prodi over his recent description of the stability pact as 'stupid'. We rapped him over the knuckles for having put in jeopardy the stability of the euro. Fortunately the financial markets know he is prone to gaffes and discounted his remark.

- an agreement on the policies governing the new European Agency for the Evaluation of Medicinal Products, which is to be based in London.

- a debate to assess the effectiveness of the measures put in place last year to fight terrorism.

In the middle of all this I was pleased to welcome to Strasbourg Adrian Sanders, MP for Torbay, who came out to lobby Commissioner Fischler for dolphin-friendly fisheries policies. The two of us impressed on the Commissioner the scale of the problem in the South West and urged him to act fast to persuade countries to change their fishing practices.

Parliament now goes into recess for a week. I will lead a Liberal delegation to the Far East to meet fellow Lib Dems in Thailand, Taiwan and South Korea and I look forward to reporting from there.

PS. I am attaching two speeches I made in Parliament this week - the first on the Stability and Growth Pact, and the second on enlargement. I hope that you find them both interesting. (*Appendix, I*)

**Tuesday 05 November**

Of all the continents, Asia is the one which holds the most potential for Liberalism. Classic Liberal struggles against autocratic governments abound, similar to those in Europe 200 years ago. In my eight years in the European Parliament I have visited Asia on 10 occasions and have taken several groups of MEPs over there with me to show them what is happening.

Last week I led a team of Liberal Democrats from Sweden, the Netherlands, Belgium and Italy to meet our LibDem counterparts in the Far East. We spent two days in Thailand with the Democratic Party, now back in opposition but fighting the populism and corruption of Thai Raksin, who is Thailand's answer to Italy's Silvio Berlusconi.

We then flew to Taiwan to meet the Democratic Progressive Party of President Chen Shui-bian and to celebrate East Asia's most thriving democracy. They are under constant threat of attack and invasion by the People's Republic of China, which is one of the world's few remaining vile communist dictatorships. Yet we in the West fall over backwards to be nice to China while shunning Taiwan. The hypocrisy of our professing adherence to democracy in this instance is staggering and does our reputation little good.

Our final two days were spent in Seoul in South Korea, another potential military flashpoint, where we joined a conference of the Council of Asian Liberals and Democrats with representatives from Japan, Taiwan, the Philippines, Indonesia, Singapore, Cambodia, Burma and Thailand.

We were hosted by President Kim Dae Jung's Millennium Democratic Party.

Kim Dae Jung's term of office is nearing its end. He has consolidated democracy and done much to fight corruption, though sadly those around him have shown less moral fibre (including two of his sons who are in jail on corruption charges). His party, which has never enjoyed an overall majority in Parliament, will go back into opposition but will continue to advocate engagement with North Korea to help them modernise and reform (and feed their people). Chen Shui-bian in Taiwan has eighteen months of his term left to run and is still full of energy, though he too faces an opposition majority in Parliament. His challenge is to maintain democracy in Taiwan and try to set an example for modernisers in continental China.

In Singapore our leader, Chee Soon Juan, is in jail. In Burma, Aung San Suu Kyi is under house arrest. Liberal Democrats in Asia are putting up a brave fight for freedom and deserve our support. International recognition is perhaps the most useful support we can give them.

**Sunday 10 November**

The European Parliament's Committee on Justice and Home Affairs voted on Tuesday to approve my report on the proposed EU readmission agreement with Hong Kong. This will now go to the floor of the House either later this month or next. Although party leaders do not normally pilot measures through the House I was prepared to break with tradition because this one is particularly important. It is the first of what will be a series of agreements between the EU and third countries about repatriation of illegal immigrants. Under the agreement, the EU will be able to require the Hong Kong government to take back any of their nationals found here without the necessary papers - and vice versa. There are of course safeguards to prevent return if the person is likely to be ill treated on their return.

Any credible immigration policy needs a credible policy of repatriation. But whereas this is relatively problem-free with Hong Kong it could be much more difficult with a country like Pakistan. My report chastises the European Commission for failing to consult Parliament while negotiations were taking place and makes our approval of the agreement conditional on the Council and the Commission making statements to Parliament followed by a debate and vote on the principles which should govern a readmission policy.

The most important news from the European Parliament this week was a deal struck with the Council which will ban all cosmetic products that have been tested using experiments on live animals. These are among the most painful tests on animals since they measure toxicity. Some 38,000 animals are used each year in Europe. The ban will come into force from 2009 and is largely the work of my North West LibDem colleague Chris Davies MEP. The final deal, under Parliament's powers of co-decision, was hammered out at 4am on Thursday between fifteen MEPs and a representative of each of the fifteen member state governments.

Among the pleasures of my week was a visit from Mike Treleaven, our Prospective Parliamentary Candidate for Totnes, and meeting a group of twenty visitors from the UK's Liberal Democrat European Group. When people come and see the European Parliament at work they get a far better 'feel' for how the EU really works.

**Friday 15 November**

Recent reports of the EU have been dominated by two issues: failure to manage the public accounts, and Cyprus. Both issues have also occupied my time. For what they may be worth, here are my views:

The reason we know about fraud against the EU budget is that the European Parliament insists on the auditors reports being published. Anti-Europeans then seize on the existence of fraud to make an anti-EU case. The grievances of recently-sacked EU budgetary official Marta Andreasen, who was dismissed for incompetence and for having lied about her previous employment record, have poured fuel on this fire.

*EU've got mail!*

Fraud is a serious problem, but the extent of fraud against the EU budget is no greater than against national or local government budgets. The EU is moving from a cash-based to an accrual-based accounting system which will help detect and prevent fraudulent claims, but this takes a number of years (the UK Government has also been doing this; we started in 1993 and the process is still not complete!). Adding to the difficulty is the fact that 50% of EU funds are dispersed by national governments, so although the European Commission is legally responsible it does not have operational control.

I believe that Commissioners Neil Kinnock and Michaele Schreyer are doing a good job sorting out the problems. But we can expect a few more years yet of headlines claiming that the EU is riddled with corruption, which is not true.

I was in Athens when the UN's proposals on Cyprus were published on Tuesday. Their wisdom lies in their being not a blueprint but a menu of formulae from which the Cypriots must choose. The only viable outcome (other than the status quo) will be some form of federal government for the island which protects the rights of the one in five Cypriots of Turkish origin and restores to some Greek Cypriots the homes from which they were expelled.

The chances of a peaceful settlement are still slim, but the carrot of EU membership for Cyprus has opened a small window of opportunity. Greek Prime Minister Costas Simitis, who I met on Wednesday morning just before his cabinet met to discuss the plan, reacted cautiously. He has to deal with nationalist elements in his own PASOK party, to say nothing of the Greek Cypriots whose newspaper headlines screamed betrayal by the UN. He told me that public opinion on the Greek side is poorly prepared for any compromise; my contacts in Brussels with Turks suggest they are little better prepared.

Key to any success will be political leadership. The leader of the new Turkish governing party, Mr Erdogan, will be in Athens on Monday. If the two of them can find the mutual courage to go out on a limb to sue for peace they may take the islanders with them. If not, there's little hope. And bringing only the Greek half of Cyprus into the EU will store up potential troubles in military terms while the economy of northern Cyprus slides further into the mire, dragging Turkey with it.

**Monday 02 December**

Air traffic delays meant that I missed a meeting with Charles Caccia MP on Monday morning. Charles is an Italian-Canadian elected as a Liberal MP in Ottawa and is a trenchant and perceptive observer of developments in immigration policy. I was sorry to miss him.

Monday afternoon and all of Tuesday saw me in Warsaw to welcome the Union for Freedom (UW) into the Liberal family. Former Solidarity leaders like Bronislaw Geremek and Wladislaw Frasyniuk (now party leader) set up this Liberal party after the revolution. They are not currently represented in Parliament, though they still have senators; but they are an intellectual powerhouse and the only evident partner for Liberals and most commentators expect to see their return in the near future. Poland needs a strong pro-European force to counter a growing scepticism about joining the EU, especially among the thousands of small farmers who dominate rural life.

On Tuesday evening I invited Adam Michnik, the editor of the newspaper Gazeta Wyborcza, and other Liberal friends to dinner. Little did I know that the restaurant which I chose had been the basement floor of the former HQ of Poland's state security police. A number of my guests had been there in past years. It was a salutary reminder of how important it is to shore up democratic freedoms through EU membership.

Back in Brussels on Wednesday I met Hanan Ashrawi MP. Her leadership of Palestinian civil society in the search for non-violent resistance to Israeli occupation is admirable. She sees little chance of peace unless Labour wins the Israeli election next month but was in Brussels to see the EU High Representative for foreign policy Javier Solana, whose peace-making efforts she values highly. In a busy day I also received visitors from Indonesia, the People's Republic of China and the German Bundestag (the newly elected Liberal MPs from our sister party, the Free Democrats). But the most enjoyable was a meeting with George Parker. Eight years ago, when I was first elected, George was a cub reporter on the Western Morning News. Now he is the head of the Brussels bureau of the Financial Times.

For some months I've been involved in a project to establish an experimental "e-parliament" in which legislators from across the world can be brought together. With the help of PA Consulting our chances of success are now looking greater. I'll try to report at greater length about this in a future newsletter.

Let me close with news that the Liberal Democrat Ball at the Park Lane Hilton on Thursday night was a great success. Over 300 people were there and a small fortune was raised for party funds. Congratulations to organisers Serena Tierney, Maureen Thomas and Vera Head.

**Friday 06 December**

I try desperately to keep Sundays as a day for my family. But if an early start is needed in Brussels on a Monday morning, as was the case this week and will be again next, I have to leave Langport after lunch on Sunday for a flight to Brussels from Bristol.

The reason this week was to address a conference on European defence policy in Bonn. There is a growing view that the EU needs to do more to provide for its own defence: we currently rely on American NATO troops and equipment for some basic needs, such as airlifting armoured vehicles. The EU (population 370 million) currently spends only half as much on defence as the US (population 250 million). We could not sustain troops in combat for any length of time without American support. And we are a long way behind in reconnaissance capability. Slowly and gingerly, Europeans are beginning to plan for how they would cope with a military action which did not enjoy US support. The EU's proposed Rapid Reaction Force, designed essentially for peacekeeping and humanitarian assistance, is part of this. My message to the conference was that we should tread softly and reassure our transatlantic partners.

Parliament's plenary session was dominated by the vexed issue of MEP's pay and allowances. The Liberal Democrat group has long argued for reform of a system in which travel to and from Brussels is reimbursed generously to compensate MEPs from southern countries whose salaries are very low (MEPs earn the same as national MPs and are paid by national governments). We propose that MEPs should be paid a common salary from the EU budget and that flight tickets should be reimbursed at cost rather than on a basis of distance travelled. German and Italian MEPs, who are the best paid, sought to block any reform and succeeded in carrying a number of others with them. We lost though more MEPs than ever before voted for the reform proposal put forward jointly by the Liberal Democrats, Communists and Greens.

The most enjoyable moment of my week was launching a book published by Austria's Styria Verlag about Europe's Right Wing Demagogues. Analysts have written chapters studying the likes of Haider, Le Pen, Bossi and Lepper. I was able to highlight the European Parliament's work against racism and xenophobia and had a rare opportunity to make a speech in German. Sadly, the book has not yet been translated into other languages. It deserves to be.

**Monday 16 December**

The European summit (or Council, at which the heads of state and government meet) in Copenhagen this weekend will decide - barring any last minute hitches - to admit ten new countries into the EU. If it works, Liberal Democrats can claim the credit. Other parties have tried to delay or derail the process by raising objections to the free movement of workers or farm produce, by claiming that the Czech Republic's wartime 'Benes' decrees are illegal or on other spurious grounds[1]. Our Liberal friends in the Danish government have held the line. Nonetheless my predecessor Pat Cox (now President of the European Parliament) was in

Cyprus, Athens and Ankara during the week and I was in Lithuania and Bulgaria trying to help solve last minute problems and reassure the candidate countries. Danish Prime Minster Anders Fogh Rasmussen was talking money with the Polish Prime Minister right up until the last moment. It's history in the making and it is fascinating.

The huge flaw in the process, however, is the failure of most of the EU's national governments to build public support for what they are doing. To me, the advantages of enlarging the EU are clear: it will stabilise new democracies and prevent them from descending into Yugoslavia-style ethnic conflict; it will add tremendously to the competitiveness of Europe's economy, helping to drive down prices; and it will help in the fight against organised crime, which is probably the most serious and urgent challenge facing democracy. Rarely do I find, however, at meetings anywhere in my constituency, people who know what the EU is doing and why.

Whatever our Presidents and Prime Ministers agree this weekend, the process will not be over. Each of the new countries except Cyprus will put the plan to its people in a referendum next year. There is already evidence of British and Danish opponents of the EU seeking to ferment dissension in the new countries through well-financed, planned campaigns for a NO vote. The EU's supporters will need to pile in too to help us win the referendum campaigns. Fancy a working holiday in Latvia?

All this opens the debate about where Europe ends. Serbia, Croatia and the other countries of the western Balkans will probably be next in line to join the EU. Soon we may receive approaches from the Ukraine, Moldova and Belarus; and possibly one day Georgia, Armenia and Azerbaijan in the southern Caucasus. My view, in a nutshell, is that if the carrot of EU membership persuades countries to entrench democracy, the rule of law and respect for human rights, as it has done in Slovakia; respect for minorities as in the Czech Republic; to fight against corruption, to improve public administration etc (i.e. to meet the criteria for EU membership) then we should accept them. If, one day, it is no longer a 'European' Union, but a wider one our capacity to solve the world's problems will have grown.

[1] *The Benes Decrees were issued after World War Two by then President of Czechoslovakia Edvard Benes to transfer ethnic Germans from the country and confiscate their property. The decrees became an issue for heated debate during negotiations on the accession of the Czech Republic to the EU.*

**Monday 23 December**

In Strasbourg this week we scored a victory for the principle that the polluter should pay when we set the seal on the Waste Electrical and Electronic Equipment (WEEE) Directive. This aims to tackle the mountain of waste, often toxic, from discarded electronic devices by putting the onus on manufacturers to pay for cleaning it up. I was involved in the issue in 1996 when I piloted through Parliament the opinion of the Economic and Monetary Affairs Committee: my concern then was to make sure that the costs fell squarely on the manufacturer and not the retailer. Altogether it has taken us seven years to get this legislation onto the statute books. It will take a further two or three years before member states put it into national law, but already companies like Sony and JVC are producing goods which are less environmentally harmful when discarded.

We also approved the EU's budget for next year which, at some 100 billion euros, is equal to just over one per cent of the EU's GDP. (National governments in the EU typically spend between thirty-five and fifty-five percent of GDP).

Most importantly for me, Parliament approved my report giving the green light to the EU's readmission agreement with Hong Kong. This commits either party to accepting the return of any of its citizens found residing illegally on the territory of the other. It is part of the EU's emerging immigration policy, and will be the first in a series of such agreements between the EU and third countries. Though Parliament has no legal power to amend the Treaty, the Commissioner accepted my recommendation that future such agreements should have a stronger clause on protection of human rights, ie. the EU should not return people where there is any danger of their being persecuted. In reality, forced departures rarely take place: voluntary return is much more common. But for immigration policy to be credible and allow us to return criminals such agreements are necessary.

Greece takes over the EU Presidency (from Denmark) on 01 January: I am pleased that one of their priorities is to develop the planned EU immigration policy foreseen in the Amsterdam Treaty of 1997. The idea that we can have zero-immigration policies has not worked; moreover it is damaging our economies and threatening our standard of living since we have a growing skills shortage. While June's Seville summit under the Spanish Presidency saw Blair and Aznar pandering to popular prejudice against immigrants, Greece's headline objective is to develop the EU as a 'community of values'. In Athens on Friday I told Prime Minister Simitis that I trusted this would apply to immigration policy in particular. I hardly needed to point out that 2002 years ago a couple of asylum seekers in Bethlehem were just as badly housed as many are today.

I will not write again until 10 January. In the meantime I wish you a peaceful winter solstice (politically correct term for Christmas) and a resolute start to the Gregorian New Year.

Graham with Members of the ELDR Group following
his election as Group Leader.
January 2002

Speaking at the launch of a book condemning
far right politics in Europe.
December 2002

Graham with European Commissioner Pascal Lamy.
March 2003

Campaigning in Poland for a Yes vote in their referendum
on EU membership.
May 2003

*ELDR Leaders' summit, Brussels Autumn 2003*
From L to R: Danish Minister Anders Fogh Rasmussen, Finnish Prime Minister Matti Vanhanen, European Commission President Romano Prodi, ELDR Group Leader Graham Watson

Graham with visitors from Thornbury, 2003

At the helm.
October 2003

At the launch of Liberal Language. With editor, Sarah Kent.
September 2003

# 2003

*The situation in Iraq was the subject of intense debate within the EU in 2003. The Union was divided between those member states broadly supporting the United States, and those opposing military action. At the forefront of the debate were the United Kingdom and Spain in the former camp, and France and Germany in the latter. Central and Eastern European countries hoping to join the EU in 2004 also cast their lot into either camp, the majority opting to support the US publicly in a letter to the press, prompting France's President Chirac to comment: "Concerning the candidate countries, honestly, I felt they acted frivolously, because entry into the European Union implies a minimum of understanding for the others. It is not well-brought up behaviour. They missed a good opportunity to keep quiet." The strong difference of opinion on this important issue led to many questioning the efficiency and worth of the EU's Common Foreign and Security Policy. The Iraq question also overshadowed the European Council summits held this year.*

*The enlargement of the EU remained at the top of the agenda of EU business in 2003, as the Commission released a series of reports on the progress of candidate countries towards accession. As a gesture of goodwill and good sense, the European Parliament invited 'Observers' from the ten candidate states to join MEPs in the conduct of Parliamentary business. The Observers were affiliated to political groups, and had the right to take part in the day-to-day work of the EP, but without the right to vote. Referenda were also taking place this year in the candidate countries to ratify their decisions to join the EU.*

*Further issues this year included the continuation of the Convention on the Future of Europe, charged with drawing up a draft EU constitution. The Convention published its draft text in time for the European Council meeting in June. The recurring themes of the Stability Pact and Parliament's Members' Statute were also ever-present, and a new scandal at the European Commission involving its statistics department, Eurostat, made the headlines and threw into question the accountability of the EU's executive.*

*The Presidency of the EU in 2003 was held by Greece and Italy.*

## Friday 10 January

The European Parliament got back to work on Monday with meetings of the political groups to prepare next week's Strasbourg plenary session. The headline debates will be on statements from the Council and Commission on Afghanistan and a statement by Greece's Prime Minister to outline the priorities of the incoming Greek Presidency of the Council. Greece is prioritising agreement on a common EU immigration and asylum policy, which the member states pledged to achieve by 2004 but which thus far remains elusive. My impression is that theirs will be an effective Presidency: six months is a short time in the Chair, but they seem well briefed and well prepared.

Other debates range from involving local and regional government more in the EU's affairs to possible harmful effects of submarine sonar on cetacean creatures (eg. whales and dolphins).

The main focus of my week was a one day conference I organised on Liberalism in Christianity and Islam. I brought together academics, journalists and politicians from Islamic and Christian communities to discuss how moderates can stop the extremists (Christian fundamentalists in Washington or Islamic or Jewish fundamentalists in the Middle East) taking us to war. Their contributions were generally fascinating; there was discussion of different concepts of freedom, of the politics of identity and of the 'secular' versus the 'religious' state. One of the speakers, Yasmin Alibhai-Brown of the Independent newspaper, quipped that dialogue with both the USA and Iraq is difficult because while Iraq is secular but not democratic, the USA is democratic but not secular. Both reflect aspects of intolerance. (I found a book about Islam by Bernard Lewis called *What went wrong?* very useful preparation). We hope to follow up the event with a conference for Muslims from the Balkan states. Meanwhile the European Parliament's Christian Democratic Group voted on Monday to oppose Turkey's entry to the EU. Our secularism is on trial and I expect the debate to continue to rage.

One or two readers replied to my last email in December suggesting that the EU should not take in new countries until it can better govern the current Union. I know that the constant barrage of criticism in the UK towards the EU is affecting even Liberal Democrats' views. Reflecting on the matter over Christmas, however, strengthened my view that the EU is actually quite well governed. It is far from perfect and there are many reforms which Liberal Democrat MEPs are pressing for (just are there are in UK government). But in view of the difficulty of getting countries to work together in the common interest - and the absence of the coercion which characterised the Warsaw Pact - I believe we have achieved and we will continue to achieve miracles. And the alternatives to a supranational approach worry me intensely.

**Friday 17 January**

Socialists in the European Parliament are calling for a Committee of Inquiry into the sinking of the "Prestige" oil tanker. Liberal Democrats sided with the right in opposing such a committee, first because the European Parliament should not be abused as a forum in which to pursue national party-political campaigns and second because the EP's Transport Committee, chaired by a Liberal Democrat, is the appropriate body to conduct an investigation. However the Spanish government is using its majority in Madrid to block any national enquiry and has forbidden state employees to give evidence to an enquiry in the Galician regional parliament. If they persist, an EU enquiry will be launched, just as one was into Foot and Mouth disease in similar circumstances. Neither Aznar nor Blair seems to recognise that when you're in a hole, you should stop digging. With France and Portugal also affected by the oil slick there would be a good case for a major investigation at EU level.

\*\*\*

As I write this I am on an aeroplane to Taipei. On Friday I will speak at a conference on human rights and democracy. Another purpose of the visit is to meet President Chen Shui-bian to discuss arrangements for a possible visit by him to address the European Parliament. Parliament has approved my suggestion that he should be invited, made after ascertaining that Belgium would grant him a visa for the purpose. The People's Republic of China is furious but seems divided about how to react. For us, it's a sign of what Liberal Democrats can achieve in power: a Liberal Democrat presidency in Taiwan, a LibDem President of the European Parliament and a LibDem government in Belgium are determined that the EU should stand up to Communist China's bullying and develop civilised relations with an island of 23 million people which is now a thriving democracy and a major trading economy. I have nothing against the mainland Chinese (indeed I am a great admirer of their culture) and no particular fondness for the islanders, but the hypocrisy of EU member states in cultivating relations with a brutal dictatorship while spurning a free democracy is intolerable.

\*\*\*

This week marked the thirtieth anniversary of the accession of the UK, Denmark and Ireland to the EC. While the Irish have got on with it, using European funds to the full and training their young people to get jobs in the EU institutions, Denmark and the UK are still engaged in bitter domestic debate about membership. A small minority in each country is waging a highly effective propaganda campaign against Europe. I do not believe that the case for withdrawal will ever command majority support in either country. Nonetheless, Liberal Democrats in the Convention on the Future of Europe (the body currently reviewing the EU treaties) have pressed for a new clause in the Treaty which would allow a member state to secede. There would need to be a "cooling off" period and the secession would require the approval of a majority of the other Member States (which would almost certainly be granted), but if it were the settled will of a people, secession would happen. There is no such provision in our current treaties, nor in the US Constitution. Having one is a vital safety valve (whatever doubts Liberals might have about the wisdom of Woodrow Wilson's doctrine of the right of all peoples to self-determination).

**Friday 24 January**

The farm lobby was out in full combat gear this week when the Commission approved Commissioner Franz Fischler's plans for CAP reform. Fischler's proposals would cut subsidies, particularly lump sum payments to wealthier farmers, and break the link between the amount produced and the subsidy paid. They are a bold step in the right direction. But the reality is that we will still be paying billions of pounds in subsidies which distort world markets and hit poorer countries hard. Even if the Council of Ministers (in this case the 15 agriculture ministers) adopts the Commission proposal - which would be little short of a miracle - Europe will still face difficulties in the World Trade talks later this year for rigging its farm produce market. And it was no surprise when the opponents of reform, principally France and Ireland, denounced the Commission's proposals as totally unacceptable. So the battle lines are again drawn, but once more it will be a war of attrition between powerful producer interests and those, including the Liberal Democrats, determined to see radical change to Europe's farm policy.

Hitherto, national governments have called the shots in the CAP dispute. And decisions need unanimous support from 15 countries. But changes under discussion in the Convention on the Future of Europe may just introduce decision making by majority vote and give the European Parliament the power of co-decision. If so, our House will become the battleground between protectionists and free traders. It will be interesting to see what line the British Tories take, since many own large tracts of land.

\*\*\*

Despite the exhortations of the Britain in Europe campaign, any UK referendum on the euro seems to have been kicked into the long grass. Tony Blair has scribbled 'too difficult' on the cover of that dossier. Whatever the verdict on the precious five economic tests agreed in an Islington restaurant with Gordon Brown, there is another test: the political test. The question is "will we win?" The answer: "probably not." This damages Blair's standing in Brussels, where his fellow Prime

*EU've got mail!*

Ministers had been prepared to give him the benefit of the doubt. But it also stores up trouble at home. Major's misery over Maastricht will look minor compared to Labour's challenge to get UK approval for the new, more federal Treaty which Giscard's convention will recommend in June. Is Labour planning a "super Thursday" referendum, a once-and-for-all plebiscite on the euro and continued membership of the EU, perhaps in 2005? Procrastination on the euro may leave them no other choice.

\*\*\*

The PR department of the European Parliament has just published a comic strip cartoon novel called "Troubled Waters", designed to explain in simple terms how Parliament works. The story revolves around fictional MEP Irina Vega, a campaigner on Parliament's environment committee who gets caught up in a web of intrigue in a 'whodunnit?' involving big companies polluting rivers. It looks a good attempt to make Parliament's arcane ways comprehensible to a wide audience, until you reach page 7 on which the heroine says "so we have to reach agreement with the Council, if necessary via a conciliation committee" - at which point my 11 year old closed the book and went back to her computer video game. Och, weel...

**Friday 31 January**

Rarely would I accuse a Prime Minister of crass stupidity. They are surrounded by senior civil servants who can normally be relied on to prevent it. Yet the joint letter to 12 major newspapers by the Prime Ministers of Spain, Portugal, the UK, Italy, Denmark, Poland, the Czech Republic and Hungary - setting out their position on Iraq - almost beggars belief. It is bad enough that the EU is deeply divided in its response to the US desire to go to war. But if eight Prime Ministers take a high profile position in support of the US they as good as invite others to go public in their opposition. Moreover their letter states 'the Iraqi regime and its weapons of mass destruction represent a clear threat to world security'. The inconvenient fact that Hans Blix and his inspectors found no evidence of such weapons appears to have passed them by.

Party leaders in the European Parliament had the rare opportunity earlier this week of a chat with Hans Blix, albeit by video-link to Washington. The excellent Mr Blix - a Swedish Liberal Party member, by the way - told us that Saddam Hussein has been unco-operative. Indeed, he mounts a pretty damning case to prove a lack of co-operation. Nonetheless the inspectors have been allowed access to the places they wanted to visit and have found no conclusive evidence of a weapons programme. Blix told us he would welcome more time. George Bush appears determined not to allow it. And the European unity which persuaded the USA last September to seek a UN Security Council resolution, rather than mount a unilateral pre-emptive strike, has evaporated. An exasperated Jo Grimmond once said of the Liberal Party 'the moment you want to use it, it turns to putty in your hands'. The same might be said now of the EU's much vaunted common foreign and security policy.

According to UNSC Resolution 1441, Iraq is required to co-operate fully with the weapons inspectors. If its failure to co-operate is so blatant that the UN Security Council deems it to put Iraq in material breach of international law, military action may be inevitable to uphold the UN's credibility. But while the inspectors are allowed to inspect and find nothing, public opinion will not be convinced. And if the Americans possess the evidence they claim, they'd better damn well publish it.

The European Parliament debated Iraq on Wednesday.

\*\*\*

First prize for 'Euromyth of the Week' must go to the story that pigs need toys. EU animal welfare provisions require that their comfort be improved with straw, sawdust, hay or wood in their stalls. I understand that the UK Government has suggested playthings in addition, and threatened reluctant farmers with fines. Farmers paying fines for forgetting a teddy bear? Labour government ministers might fly!

\*\*\*

In Berlin one day this week to brief the German Free Democrat (Liberal) MPs on the goings on in Brussels, I expressed the hope that they would poll more that five per cent in next year's European elections. That way they would overcome the hurdle which currently denies them representation in the European Parliament (they polled 4.7% last time). But I delivered a critical message. To succeed, I told them, they need to encompass the three historical strands of Liberalism: classical Liberalism (human rights, the dignity of the individual, etc); economic Liberalism (after Adam Smith) and social Liberalism. The FDP sometimes appears to represent only economic Liberalism, ceding social Liberalism and occasionally even classical Liberalism to the Green Party. Economic Liberalism is in fashion almost everywhere. The FDP's weakness should be a warning that we ignore the other traditions at our peril.

Happy campaigning!

**Thursday 06 February**

Oh, dear! The trickle of joint letters from heads of state and government risks becoming a regular stream. Last week I reported about a joint letter by eight of them on Iraq which blew a hole in Europe's so-called 'common foreign policy'. This unhealthy trend towards the dumping of prime ministerial problems in somebody else's letterbox has continued with a letter this week from Blair, Chirac and Schroeder to the Greek presidency of the EU calling for 'radical measures' to boost economic competitiveness. They call for "Europe to match words with actions".

The facts are as follows:

- France has the highest deficit rate for failure to implement single market legislation, at 3.8% when the Barcelona target was 1.5%; Germany has a deficit rate of 2.7%;

- the deficit rate in France and Germany has widened in the last six months;

- France and Germany have respectively 14 and 10 Directives which are more than two years overdue in implementation, the worst record in the EU;

- France has the worst record in the EU for infringements, at 216 cases open. Germany is third with 143 (behind Italy, UK is 8th with 107);

- France and Germany have been among the chief culprits in blocking agreement on the Community Patent, still blocked one year on from Barcelona;

- Germany and UK have just reached an unholy alliance to seek changes to the Takeover Bids Directive which could block it.

The hypocrisy of the Leaders of the EU's three major economies in blaming "Europe" for their own failure to act is breathtaking. But maybe that's politics. The sad reality is that the failure of France, Germany and sometimes the UK to carry out the economic reforms they agreed three years ago has meant that Europe is still far from economic health.

\*\*\*

Simon Hughes, MP and Baroness Thomas of Wallisdown were among thirty portfolio holders from Liberal Democrat groups in national parliaments who came to Brussels this week for a briefing on Justice and Home Affairs issues. This is the first of a series of conferences, one for each policy area, which I have designed to try to improve co-operation between MPs and MEPs. I hope to make them an annual event as part of my drive to "bring Europe closer to the people". Well, to the people's national representatives, at least.

\*\*\*

Next week in Strasbourg we will debate a report on drug dependence. It approves new moves in public health policy which begin - at long last - to treat drug addicts as sick people rather than criminals. Lib Dems have tabled amendments to ensure that voluntary workers offering shelter to addicts do not thereby render themselves liable to criminal charges, as was the case recently in East Anglia. In this area at least, policy is moving in the right direction.

Finally, this will be the last newsletter you will receive for the next few weeks, due to the selection process for PEPCs[1] - we'll be back in mid-March.

---

[1] *The process by which the Liberal Democrats selected their candidates for the 2004 elections to the European Parliament forbade certain forms of canvassing by those seeking selection. It was deemed by the Returning Officer that my newsletters might constitute such canvassing.*

## Friday 21 March

Some quick foot-work last week prevented another incursion into civil liberties in the fight against terrorism. The USA has demanded that European airlines provide all sorts of information on passengers flying across the Atlantic: credit card details, information on lifestyle preference (from airline loyalty cards), eating habits, income bracket etc. Normally the EU will not share such data with the USA since the latter has no data protection legislation to speak of and the information could end up in many hands, not just those of government agencies. This time the European Commission, under pressure from the EU Member States to co-operate with the US, and from the airline industry, was inclined to give in. Liberal Democrat MEPs forced onto Parliament's agenda a discussion of the matter, but the new Chairman of Parliament's Justice and Home Affairs Committee (a Spanish right winger) moved to have the issue taken off. As a former Chair of the committee I believed I had the authority to challenge him. I succeeded not only in securing the debate, but in ensuring a resolution condemning the Commission's approach and calling for resistance to American demands. It is hardly a great triumph, but it means the USA will have to pay a little more respect to Europe's concerns to protect its citizens. Our data protection legislation is quite good, even if too frequently flouted.

\*\*\*

Dominating our agenda this week has been Iraq. The row between the UK and France has plumbed new depths of mutual mudslinging. Britain has used its UN veto far more often than France, and Jack Straw's attack on the French brought a tough private phone call from his opposite number in Paris. I do not share the apocalyptic view that this spells the end of the UN or the end of the EU, but the heads of state and government will need to rebuild bridges at their meeting this weekend in Brussels. If they've any sense they'll stick to the summit's pre-planned agenda of economic reform and not let positions on Iraq poison their gathering.

\*\*\*

Next week I welcome Hong Kong's veteran civil rights campaigner Martin Lee QC to Brussels. He is still concerned about the implementation of Article 23 of the territory's Basic Law, which could undermine political freedoms. My view is that the People's Republic of China is proceeding cautiously vis-à-vis Hong Kong, but their implacable opposition to democratic Taiwan leaves little hope for the longer term. My initiative to have Taiwanese President Chen Shui-Bian invited to the European Parliament was shot down in flames when Belgium's Liberal government had to retreat from its plan to issue him a visa under massive pressure from the PRC and from other EU governments. China's bullying knows few bounds.

## Friday 28 March

In eight years in the European Parliament I have not known such hostility to the anglo-saxon world. John Major's infamous period of "non-cooperation with the EU" (after the ban on BSE-contaminated British Beef) and accusations two years ago that the UK and the USA were spying on EU member states through the Echelon information-gathering system gave rise to reactions which were as nothing compared to the opposition to the war in Iraq. Whatever else Tony Blair has or has not done, he has convinced his European colleagues that, when it comes to the crunch, the UK is with America and not Europe.

Not that reactions to France's position are at all warm. Chirac is roundly condemned for his disparaging remarks about the accession countries of Central and Eastern Europe, some of whom voiced support for war. And the intensity of the war of words between London and Paris causes despair. If one idea is gaining ground it is that Britain and France should no longer be allowed to pursue independent foreign policy lines. For while Europe is divided, America holds sway. The war in Iraq might yet presage a much more united EU foreign policy. After all, if we negotiate through one person (the European Commissioner for External Trade) in the WTO, why not one EU seat at the U.N Security Council? [The views of those who have attacked me for advocating this idea publicly have helped to convince me it must be right!]

Last weekend's EU summit was almost but not totally eclipsed by the war. These Spring economic summits have been held, in addition to the twice-yearly European Council (the formal name for the meeting of our heads of state and heads of government), for three years now, since the Lisbon Council under the Portuguese Presidency decided on a ten year programme 'to give Europe the most competitive, dynamic, knowledge-based economy in the world'. No mean feat! Three years into the ten, too little progress has been made. But in a development utterly lost in the media coverage of war, our leaders actually agreed last weekend that by 2010 renewable energy should supply 22% of our electricity needs and bio-fuels 5.75% of our transport fuel. Moreover, they agreed to a tax on carbon energy and an action plan on environmental technologies to help meet the Kyoto targets.

Some progress on environmental issues in the European Parliament, too. A report by my Lib Dem colleague Elspeth Attwooll, MEP for Scotland, which was adopted on Thursday, makes the "finning" of sharks illegal. Those European fishermen who have been cutting the fins off sharks to sell them to the lucrative Chinese market will henceforth do so at their peril. Time now to get enough inspectors on duty to make sure a few early prosecutions help to 'encourager les autres'.

## Friday 04 April

The EU's national governments have moved quickly to patch up their differences over Iraq. Germany sent torpedo boats to defend American ships in the Mediterranean and France has accepted US administration of Iraq after the war, until the UN can be brought in. But Colin Powell's visit to Brussels did little to quell the worries of European countries' foreign affairs ministers that America seems keen to pick a fight with Syria and Libya too. With Afghanistan not yet totally under control, the US could find itself fighting a war across a large swathe of the Muslim world, in which many more underemployed young Arab men sign up as crusaders for a holy war.

One effect of all this has been to relaunch with fervour the debate about an EU defence policy. Though the UK is the only EU country spending anything like enough on defence to make this credible at present (almost 3% of GDP, compared to half that in some of the other Member States), Belgium has already put the issue firmly on the agenda by convening a conference to discuss EU security. And the recent start of the EU's first peacekeeping mission in Macedonia - where we have taken over from NATO - is tangible evidence of ability to co-operate. The European Parliament will adopt on 09 April a report drawn up at our initiative, which calls for a common defence policy. The French MEP who wrote it, former military General Phillipe Morillon, carries a lot of clout in the EU's capital cities.

\*\*\*

Finance Ministers kept their nerve on Thursday and left euro interest rates unchanged despite a weakening economy. Again, Gordon Brown was excluded from an important meeting because the UK stays out of the euro. The cost of this is ever higher, with Britain's share of inward investment continuing to fall. At a lunch I chaired for UK MEPs from all parties on Wednesday with Unilever, their Chairman Richard Greenhalgh told us that if no decision is taken on British membership of the euro in the next parliament, Unilever companies will be investing heavily elsewhere.

I believe the best bet for Blair now is to put together with the June 2004 euro elections a referendum on euro membership and a referendum to ratify the new EU Treaty, which will emerge from Giscard's Convention on the Future of Europe. I have never been totally sure that the UK will remain in the EU long term, but such a super-Thursday type poll would at least force the sane among us to wage one hell of a campaign. Those who were defeated in the 1975 referendum but have never accepted the outcome might then finally be silenced. Until then I've no doubt the United Kingdom Independence Party (UKIP) will continue to field candidates, including many for the local elections this May.

**Friday 11 April**

In Strasbourg this week for our monthly 'plenary' session the most important business was the voting on the accession treaties for ten new member states. We voted them one by one and approved them all with substantial majorities. All had over 500 votes in favour, but 80 members (mostly German and Austrian) refused to vote for the Czech Republic in protest at wartime decrees confiscating property, which, although in disuse, have never formally been repealed. (The Czech Government has of course officially declared them to be no longer valid). Interestingly, most French MEPs voted against the new countries, probably pandering to a protectionist agricultural lobby at home. I'm proud to report that Liberal Democrats were the only party in the House to vote 100% in favour of all the new countries. None of my 53 MEPs voted against or abstained on any of the countries wishing to join. On 16 April the heads of state and government of the 15 will meet in Athens to sign their agreement to the new members and on 01 May Parliament will welcome 'observer' MEPs. This leaves one year for referenda and parliamentary ratification in the ten new member countries (only Cyprus has no referendum) before they join officially on 01 May 2004. What makes this enlargement different from any previous one is the historic reunification of a continent divided for so long by the Yalta settlement after WW2. The sense of occasion in the Chamber was tremendous as a page of history was turned.

The referendum campaigns in the new countries are going well. Malta and Slovenia have already voted yes. Hungary, where I was campaigning for a yes vote again last week, will vote on Saturday (12 April). On 22 April and again on 06 May I'll be out on the stump in Slovakia, which votes on 16 May, while other Lib Dem MEPs have campaigned in Lithuania (11 May). Can a foreign MEP who speaks not a word of their languages make a difference? I believe we can. At the very least our presence ensures that our sister parties are out campaigning and the media coverage we receive is good.

\*\*\*

In other votes this week we approved (and slightly increased) the budget for the new member countries and called on the member states to adopt an EU defence policy. As I spoke in the defence debate on Wednesday afternoon my press officer sent in through an usher a note with the breaking news of the fall of Baghdad, which I was able to announce to the House. What a relief!

The one-week Easter recess approaches, and local election campaigning. My next missive will be after Easter. Happy canvassing!

## Monday 28 April

I spent barely 36 hours in Brussels last week, but still had to fit in all my normal work there.

Easter Monday saw me out on the doorsteps in Bath in the local election campaign, then flying to Bratislava to spend Tuesday campaigning for a Yes vote in Slovakia's referendum campaign to join the EU. Our Lib Dem party there, the Alliance for a Free Citizen (ANO) is campaigning hard; but they need at least 50% of the electorate to vote to give it validity. Slovaks go to the polls on 17 May, a week after the Lithuanians.

On Wednesday and Thursday morning I was in Brussels, where Parliament's budgetary control committee was setting the standards we require the Commission to meet if they want us to sign off the EU's accounts next year. Much of the European Parliament's power is in budgetary matters. My Danish Liberal Democrat colleague Ole Sorensen is giving the Commission a hard time, and rightly so, over the slow pace of accounting reform. Neither Parliament nor the auditors have found evidence of fraud, but the much mis-quoted Commission "whistleblower" Marta Andreasen said she believed the systems to be vulnerable to it.

On Thursday Robin Teverson (my former Lib Dem MEP colleague) joined me for a meeting with the head of the European Investment Fund. Robin now runs Finance Cornwall, a £60 million fund which helps small businesses with loan and venture capital under the EU's structural funds (Objective 1). We want to do the same in Objective 2 areas but the EIF has not yet approved it. Their statutes require them to make a return on their capital and they feel already over-exposed to the UK small business market. Yet if they do not give us the go-ahead by July we will be unable to use all the Objective 2 funding available. There is a contradiction here between the requirements of policy delivery and the requirement on the EIF to show a return. I believe I'll have to call in the regional policy commissioner, Michel Barnier.

On Thursday afternoon I addressed the Wyndham Place Charlemagne Trust in London on 'God in the EU Constitution'. I was pitted against the leader of the Catholic Church (well, actually not the Pope himself, but the head of the European Catholic Bishops' Conference). I won the vote in the straw poll which closed the meeting, which suggests either you do not always need God on your side or that He too may be convinced of the need for a secular state.

Friday, Saturday, Sunday and Monday have seen me on the doorsteps again; in Bournemouth, North Wiltshire, Bristol, South Gloucestershire, Taunton Deane, Torbay and Mid Devon. My feeling is that Lib Dems are set to do well in these elections. I've never known Tory morale quite so low.

Keep your fingers crossed for good results on 01 May.

Happy campaigning.

## Tuesday 06 May

Last week I led a delegation of Asian and European MPs to Cambodia to campaign with our Liberal sister party the Sam Rainsy Party and - by implication - to warn Cambodia's government that the SRP has powerful foreign friends who will not take kindly to government intimidation of its opponents. I reproduce below a short article I have written about the visit.

\*\*\*

Visits to former Central and Eastern European countries shortly to join the EU remind me of their liberation from communist rule during the cold war. Yet the real horrors of communism are now hardly seen in most of these countries. A visit to Cambodia is a salient reminder of the inhumanity of a dangerous dogma.

In July, Cambodians go to the polls to pass judgement on the latest five year government of Hanoi-backed Hun Sen and his Cambodian People's Party. While the 1988 elections were far from perfect there was at least a measure of democracy. Some further progress has been made since then. Yet despite the country's almost total dependence on western aid, donor countries have failed to secure conditions for a genuinely free and fair election this year. America is pushing the government hard for respect for human rights; the EU is doing much less, despite being the larger donor.

Why? Are we trying to curry favour to increase our influence at the expense of the USA? Or is it simply that US evangelism fights harder for the oppressed than the EU's don't-rock-the-boat-style christian-social democracy?

Perhaps, as one diplomat in Phnom Penh suggested to me, things have now calmed down to an 'acceptable level' of violence and intimidation. To an Ulsterman like the gentleman in question, this may hold some appeal; to those concerned for the safety of the country's opposition politicians, there can be no 'acceptable' level of violence.

Of the EUR 24 million that the EU will invest in Cambodia this year, less than EUR 400,000 will be spent on promoting democracy and human rights. Most will go to projects which are government backed. Valuable projects, no doubt, included de-mining and rehabilitating street children; but in some cases projects from which the regime will cream off money through corruption. A decade of massive overseas aid has seen far less tangible improvement than such money would have produced in an EU accession country.

A fortnight ago a 42 year old judge was gunned down in broad daylight by a motorcycle pinion rider. The culprits are unlikely to be found. Nobody has yet been arrested for the recent same style killing of human rights activist Om Radsady. In the case of an opposition Sam Rainsy Party activist, the man's nephew has been jailed after having 'confessed' in police custody that he accidentally shot his uncle; freed from police custody, he claims that his uncle was the victim of a gun toting motorcycle pinion rider. The circumstances are likely identical to those of the two cases above. The state authorities shrug their shoulders. Intimidation of political opponents in a climate of impunity is a powerful way of holding on to power. As Burma's Aung San Suu Kyi said, it is not power which corrupts, but the fear of losing power.

The Council of Asian Liberals and Democrats, Asia's most effective cross-border political network, is not standing idly by. Politicians from Sri Lanka, the Philippines, Thailand, Singapore and Taiwan are lending their support to Cambodia's opposition Leader Sam Rainsy in his attempt to clean up the country. Despite the intimidation of his supporters he may yet gain over one third of the vote, which is enough under Cambodia's unusual constitution to hold the government to account. The collapse of support for government coalition partner FUNCINPEC, the former royalist party - seen in the huge crowds attracted to Sam Rainsy rallies in rural areas - could yet allow this former finance minister and his overseas Khmer exile backers to force some of his much touted '100 measures' on to the agenda of government.

Expatriates working in Phnom Penh fear violence, perhaps civil war, if the opposition wins too many votes. Better the limited stability of today than a return to the years of violence, many argue. Yet civil society, in the form of the voters, seems more mature than Cambodia's political party establishment. They want freedom and justice and a democracy mature enough to cope with a change of political leadership. It may not happen this time, but my bet is on Rainsy being Prime Minister by 2008. The aid-giving countries should be careful not to retard the will for change.

Victims of the Khmer Rouge regime, who have awaited justice for nearly twenty five years, are not content with a government which seeks to frustrate the United Nations in its attempts to set up a tribunal while some of the architects of those abuses live, as do the current killers, in impunity. Despite grinding levels of poverty and high rates of infant mortality, illiteracy and disease, the Cambodian people preserve their dignity. And they demand respect.

**Friday 09 May**

It was a much larger group of Liberal Democrat MEPs which met in Brussels this week to prepare next week's Strasbourg plenary session. In addition to our 53 members hitherto we welcomed 13 'observer MEPs' from the Central and Eastern European countries due to join the Union on 01 May 2004. These observers, appointed from their national parliaments, will be able to take part in the work of parliament's committees and to sit with us in meetings of the full house but not to vote. Uniquely among the political groups, Liberal Democrats have decided to give them full rights in our group meetings except voting on amendments we table to primary legislation. We've worked so much with them in recent years that they are already part of the family and we hope many of them will be elected in May of next year as full members.

\*\*\*

Green issues are top of our agenda next week. Toine Manders MEP, a Dutch Liberal colleague, is parliament's rapporteur for a draft directive on Environmental Liability (making the polluter pay). The

*EU've got mail!*

Commission's proposal upset industry because they think it will cost them too much and upset the environmentalists for not going far enough. So the Commission probably got it about right. Toine does not share this view, however, and he brought through the Legal Affairs committee a text, which is friendlier to business interests, including a proposal to develop public liability insurance, which will please the financial services industry. Sadly he failed to win over his own colleagues and our Group has decided to table a series of amendments to the report of one of our own members; they are inspired mainly by our environmentalists.

The Commission also published this week a revised proposal on chemicals testing. There are over 50,000 chemicals in daily use, which have never been tested. Some of them, the so-called 'gender benders' for example, are known to interfere with life forms; the gender of molluscs and other aquatic creatures can be changed by exposure to chemicals in marine paints. An earlier plan to start testing and licensing them was shot down in flames by national governments as being far too onerous; the current proposal is a little more modest, but still moves us in the right direction.

Methods used to attack the Commission's proposals are fascinating. First, business sponsored the animal rights lobby to mount an attack, on the basis that testing of 50,000 chemicals would involve more experiments on live animals. Now the plan is being attacked from the USA as a trade barrier in disguise, with US businesses worried they would have to meet environmental standards, which are not required in America. I think Parliament will be supportive of the plan for a programme to test chemicals, but I expect to see the German industrial lobby (many of their 99 christian and social democratic MEPs) in full swing once our debate starts.

\*\*\*

The EU faces the interesting prospect of a crisis in the Council of Ministers. On 01 July, Italy is due to take over the six-monthly rotating Presidency of the Union. Yet Silvio Berlusconi, due to be our President-in-Office, is on trial for attempting to bribe judges in a business affair. How Europe reacts will be a revealing test of our European 'area of freedom, security and justice'.

**Saturday 17 May**

I do not often read the Daily Telegraph. British Airways normally offers its passengers only the Telegraph and the Mail, however, and on my way back from campaigning in Poland's euro referendum on Friday I succumbed. I am horrified by how far it has fallen. An article on page 12 about the euro states brazenly that UK mortgage rates are lower than those in the euro zone, which is simply untrue. In fact, the reverse is the case. An article on the following page about the Convention on the future of Europe tells its readers that Britain has only one member on the Convention, Gisela Stuart MP. We also have David Heathcoat-Amory MP, Peter Hain, Andrew Duff MEP, Lord Stockton MEP, a Labour MEP and Lord Maclennan of Rogart (though Bob is technically only a substitute member). There are others too, though I cannot from memory recall who. Moreover the Secretary to the Convention is Sir John Kerr, a high-ranking foreign office mandarin. I know the journalist who wrote the article and he is well aware of this falsehood, though I suspect the sub-editors might have doctored his text. If our broadsheet newspapers are now this bad, what hope of any reasonable public debate? (I have occasionally in the past written letters to the editor of the Daily Telegraph where I have queried their angle on developments; I do not recall that any of them has been printed.)

\*\*\*

Parliament voted by a narrow margin this week to give a second reading to the Environmental Liability Directive of which I wrote last week. The UK Tories voted against. Twenty-seven years after the Seveso incident (chemical factory fire in northern Italy) which occasioned it, we are finally getting round to taking liability seriously. Between now and second reading we have to get the balance between business and environmental interests right to ensure good legislation.

\*\*\*

Absence of proper parliamentary oversight is still a problem. EU negotiators in Brussels have initialled the text of an agreement with the USA on extradition of people suspected of serious crime, including terrorism. The European Parliament has not been consulted, though the Treaties specify that we should be. Officially, the ministers who deal with these matters are each accountable to their national parliaments. However the Conseil d'Etat in France has just refused a demand from the Assemblée Nationale that they be allowed scrutiny of it, on the basis that it is a Community agreement. Are the 15 national government ministers who will sign this off to be completely free from parliamentary oversight? Though the draft of the new constitutional treaty would give the EP new powers to reject such measures (which we do not currently enjoy), present arrangements are disgracefully lax and could mean, for example, that EU governments would surrender EU citizens to be held without trial in Guantanamo Bay, where a few already languish.

As I travel between speaking engagements in Warsaw and Dulverton on Exmoor I reflect on how democracy is valued far more highly by those who have recently known alternative forms of government. What can we do to inspire our citizens with its virtues? Answers on an electronic postcard, please.

**Friday 23 May**

'Cohesion policy' is the name we give to EU regional funding programmes, which are a very modest re-distribution of taxpayers' money from the richer to the poorer regions of Europe. (The EU budget is 1.07 percent of GDP; of this, regional funding takes up about one third. The US Federal budget, by comparison, is 24% of their GDP and redistribution is very significantly greater in monetary terms.) When Europe's 15 regional development ministers met in Greece last week they started to grapple with the consequences for regional policy in western Europe when we bring ten poorer central and eastern european countries into the EU next year. Five months after the Commission's proposals were launched, a consensus is starting to emerge about the future of regional policy, for the period 2007-2013. Aid will still go primarily to the poorest regions. It now seems highly likely, however, that regions which lose Objective 1 status (ie with a per capita income less than 75% of the EU average) as a result of statistical changes due to enlargement of the EU will get a transitional aid package. Beyond that, opinions vary. The overall budget, the share allocated to non-Objective 1 regions, the degree of de-centralisation or re-nationalisation of the policy are all issues for further debate. The Commission wants one third of the overall package to go to Objective 2 regions (income per head of between 75% and 100% of the EU average). Britain and the Netherlands want the whole package to go to the ten new countries. All agree, however, that the cohesion policy has been a success.

The Ministers will meet again in Rome on 03 October. The chairmen of the English Regional Development Agencies will no doubt continue to follow government instructions and argue in Brussels for re-nationalisation of aid policy (though top marks to our own Juliet Williams, the new South West RDA chair, who resisted the pressure during their recent meeting with Commissioner Barnier).

\*\*\*

I've been in Ankara this week trying to make sense of the contradictions in Turkey. The modernists want EU membership but face huge obstacles ensuring respect for the reform laws they've passed: for example, torture in police stations is now outlawed so the police take their hapless victims to derelict buildings instead. The Defence Minister insists the Army is changing, but it is said to have little real power over it; and the middle classes respect the army more than the politicians. EU aid to Turkey has increased a lot but is still very little on a per capita basis. Prime Minister Erdogan, who received me on Wednesday, is clearly struggling to hold together his governing AK party, most of whose MPs have no previous parliamentary experience. The reformers say they can only succeed if we first give them a firm date for EU entry; yet unless they reform they will never fulfil the (Copenhagen) criteria needed for this. These people are modern, secular democrats, but their country has a long way still to travel.

## Monday 02 June

While Fisheries Ministers met in Brussels on Monday and failed to gather the necessary collective courage to address seriously the decline in fish stocks, I was again in Poland campaigning with our sister party Unia Wolnosci (Union for Freedom) for a yes vote in their EU referendum on 08 June. Three of my MEP colleagues had been there in the previous four days. My visit took me to Lublin and to nearby Lubartow where I spoke to students at a local college and then led them like the pied piper of Hamlin, fired up with enthusiasm, to come street campaigning with me. Younger voters are very keen on EU membership, the old less so. They need a 50% turnout for the referendum to be valid. Since Poland has as many inhabitants as the rest of the new countries put together it is hugely important.

\*\*\*

In London on Tuesday night I addressed an august gathering at the Institute of Civil Engineers. They told me months ago they wanted to hear something about the EU and I had chosen the theme of Europe's new constitution, unaware at the time that on the day of my speech there would be headlines about the end of a thousand years of British history (which in itself shows a pretty poor knowledge of history)[1]. The right wing in English politics has not been so clueless about any major development since the Union of the Crowns in 1603. Then, as now, their inability to think in new ways about sovereignty threatened to jeopardise the country's vital interests.

The fact is that the proposed Constitution, published on Monday and Tuesday, is more than the 'tidying up exercise' which the government claims but far less than the radical new development claimed by the Tory euro opponents. Our Party's position that we must wait and see what the final version contains before deciding on a referendum is perfectly logical but politically weak. If Paddy[2] could argue for a referendum on the Euro (which I told him at the time was a daft idea since it could make currency management impossible in the run up to voting day and therefore cost the taxpayer millions), why cannot we say legitimately that we need a debate on the issues contained in a new EU Treaty which will, in all probability, abrogate all previous treaties?

\*\*\*

The European Parliament may finally be getting round to agreement on a proposal for MEPs pay and allowances to recommend to the national governments who decide these matters. Liberal Democrats have long argued that there should be a common rate of pay for MEPs (currently we are paid the same as national MPs from our respective countries) and that we should be reimbursed our travel expenses on the basis of actual cost rather than a fixed amount per kilometre travelled. In an era of low cost airlines the latter is indefensible (though it makes less difference to me, travelling from Bristol airport where there is no competition on the route). We vote on the issue next week. If we reach agreement, which is still far from sure, we'll be accused of voting for a pay rise. If we do not, we'll be accused of failing to clean up our act. Either way we must be on the gravy train, even though my former colleagues in the private sector are now earning five times what I earn. Hey, ho ….

\*\*\*

Thank you to those readers who replied with answers to my 'answers on an electronic postcard' plea about how to interest people in politics. Apart from the normal brickbats about how if politicians were not so corrupt, people would vote for them (why on earth do you imagine we are any different from the rest of you???), there were some very interesting responses. The one I liked most was the plea for radical policies; I agree that many people are deterred from voting because they think that the parties offer only different shades of grey. (Recent policy developments in our own party should lead us to some serious thinking here.) Making voting easier helps increase turnout, as South Somerset's experience on 01 May showed[3]. Of the other ideas I liked most the suggestion that European awareness is alive and kicking, as shown by the interest in the Eurovision song contest!

\*\*\*

*EU've got mail!*

I travel to Strasbourg this week so will not be able to attend the South West consultation seminar on cohesion policy in Plymouth on Tuesday 3rd. This conference will discuss the Treasury's proposal to do away with EU regional funding in the UK. If any of our councillors can attend to argue for a continuation of EU structural fund support for Cornwall, Devon, parts of Somerset and parts of Bristol it would be much appreciated.

[1] *Headlines in the tabloid press read:*
*'Arrogant contempt for our basic rights,' Daily Mail, 27 May 2003.*
*'Bye-bye Britain,' Daily Telegraph leader, 27 May 2003.*

[2] *Paddy Ashdown, leader of the Liberal Democrats 1989-1999.*

[3] *South Somerset was the only district in the county to operate a pilot postal/electronic/internet vote scheme during the May local elections. Turnout in this district was 46.9% compared to an average 36.85% in the rest of the county.*

## Monday 09 June

One development which is unlikely to hit the headlines is an agreement finalised this week between the European Parliament, the European Commission and the European Council on better lawmaking. It is nonetheless important. Parliament will have a new power to 'call back' legislation, particularly if we do not like the way the Commission is implementing it. And Member States will have to publish a record of how well they comply with the laws their Ministers have agreed to in Brussels - something they resisted fiercely until the very last minute of the talks. These and other provisions should make a considerable difference to the transparency and functioning of legislation, yet it has taken our negotiators (including my colleague Nick Clegg MEP) nearly two years of talks to achieve it.

\*\*\*

As I had hoped, the European Commission has well and truly rubbished David Blunkett's proposal for keeping asylum seekers in camps outside the EU while their claims are processed. In its communication 'Towards more accessible, equitable and managed asylum systems' it points out that the UK proposals raise a number of questions, the most basic being whether these Transit Processing Centres would complement or substitute current asylum arrangements. Examination is required, the Commission says, as to whether such centres are compatible with existing legislation, national law, the law of the countries hosting such centres and the European Convention on Human Rights. This is diplo speak for "No, they are not compatible". Current law requires us to offer "effective protection", which requires physical security, a guarantee against refoulement, access to asylum procedures, primary healthcare and primary education and access to a means of subsistence. The Commission document does continue, however, to propose a number of very sensible measures covering co-operation with countries of origin and transit, common reception facilities, local integration and resettlement in the EU and help with voluntary repatriation. The Commission is insisting that Member States continue to distinguish between immigration and asylum.

\*\*\*

So, did we vote ourselves a £17,000 pay rise, as reported in the UK press?[1] No. We have no power to do so. MEPs salaries are set by national governments in the Council. However, the Council had asked Parliament to come up with a proposal for a common statute for MEPs. Currently we are all paid the same as our national MPs, which means that the Austrian MEPs earn nearly four times as much as the Spanish. What the EP voted this week is a proposal that MEPs should receive a common salary from the date of the entry into force of the new constitutional treaty (i.e. probably 2008). That salary should be 50% of the salary of a judge at the European Court of Justice (this is a common EU yardstick: for example, the Ombudsman earns 65% of a judge's salary). At the same time, the current mileage-based system of travel expenses should be replaced by reimbursement of the price shown on the ticket. My Lib Dem Colleagues and I were among 167 MEPs who voted against the proposal. Why? Because we insist on a move to actual cost of reimbursement of travel from the start of parliament's new term next year; and because the proposal envisaged MEPs paying only an EU tax rate, i.e. about 10% of salary. In our view we should pay the same rate as the people we represent. Moreover, an amendment was carried out which means MEPs from the new Member States would have to wait up to ten years before qualifying for the "common salary". I would be surprised if the Council agreed to this proposal. Which was probably the intention all along of the German, Italian, Austrian and French MEPs who pushed it through.

[1] 'MEP pay overtakes Westminster' The Times, 02 June 2003.
'MEPs vote for an ever longer gravy train with a salary rise to £73,000' The Guardian, 05 June 2003.

### Friday 13 June

Commissioner Fischler's proposals for reform of the Common Agricultural Policy seem to be battling against heavy weather. A deal struck this week between France and Germany means that Germany will support France in watering down the proposals in exchange for French support for German interests in other areas. Yet the costs of keeping the CAP - in terms of taxpayer subsidies to the production and export of crops, damage to farming in developing countries and distortion of trade - continue to rise. Sometime soon we will have to grasp the nettle and transform the CAP into a common rural policy. It looks as if it will be later rather than sooner.

\*\*\*

Gordon Brown's announcement on Monday that the UK will delay entry to the Euro means the government has once again ducked the issue. Though the Chancellor announced a bill to pave the way for a referendum, no date has been set. So we will continue to pay higher prices and costlier mortgages and to lose foreign direct investment. Even though the exchange rate between the pound and the euro is now about right. Labour is running scared of a referendum on Europe. And Gordon Brown's private ambition (to be the Prime Minister who takes us in) is allowed to ride roughshod over the national interest. Tony Blair is a poor strategist.

\*\*\*

The Convention on the Future of Europe has now almost finished its work. Giscard d'Estaing will present to EU heads of state and government on Thursday a draft text. I think it is a good one. It lays down clearly in a legal text a bill of rights for EU citizens and the powers of the EU institutions. It says which powers can be exercised in Brussels and which are rightly the province of national governments and explains how decisions are to be taken in policy areas where competences are shared between government at national and EU level. After hearing the views of the EU summit and the European Parliament (debate next Wednesday) the Convention will prepare a final draft for discussion by our Prime Ministers in the autumn. Britain ought to have a referendum on it.

\*\*\*

Some of my readers have commented that I seem to spend a lot of time abroad. As Leader of the Liberal Group in the European Parliament I have a very wide brief and inevitably a lot of travelling. But most weeks I spend Friday and Saturday doing constituency engagements. I just don't write about them. Should I?

### Friday 20 June

Since accusations of "massive fraud" in the European Commission once again dominate the headlines of the UK's anti-european press, here are the facts:- Allegations concerning Eurostat, the EU's statistics office, cover several cases. Some are well known to Parliament, others less so. All date back to the period before 2000, ie during the tenure of Jacques Santer as Commission President. Following critical comments made by the Court of Auditors at that time, Parliament asked the OLAF (Office pour la Lutte Anti-Fraude or the anti-fraud Office) to investigate. They have nearly completed their investigations. In March of this year they forwarded a file to the French Prosecution service about the French director of Eurostat, Mr Franchet, and it is this which has hit the headlines. Mr Franchet is accused of syphoning money into a bank account which was not publicly declared. There is no suggestion that the money was used for personal enrichment, but it was clearly irregular.

At a hearing in Parliament's budgetary control committee on Tuesday Commissioners Schreyer (budgets), Kinnock (personnel) and Solbes (statistical unit, inter alia) all gave evidence. The extent to which they are responsible for a situation inherited from the past depends to my mind on whether they failed to act, if they knew of the problems. It is clear that many of the problems have been sorted out by the financial and administrative reforms of the last two years and by additional Commission action following pressure from Parliament in granting discharge for the 2001 budget. However the Commissioners claim they were unaware of the OLAF investigation into this Eurostat bank account. This may be true: OLAF is a body independent of the European Commission. But why has it taken three years since the start of the OLAF investigations in 2000 for Commissioners to become aware of possible irregularities in one of the Commission's departments? And had they, as Eurostat's director claims, been informed by him and approved of his actions? Therein lies the heart of the investigation by our budgetary control committee. The issue raises serious questions about accounting practices and political accountability. It seems highly unlikely to me that it involves fraud. But expect more headlines. Because the pressure has been so great that the Commission's internal auditor, Jules Muis, yesterday announced he will not seek re-appointment next year when his contract comes up for renewal.

While on the subject of money and politics, Parliament voted on Thursday to approve a proposal by the Council of Ministers for limited state funding of European political parties. If a party has MEPs from at least a quarter of the EU member states and has polled at least three per cent of the vote in those countries it qualifies as a European political party for funding purposes. It can in addition receive private donations up to a maximum value of 12,000 euros per donation, but any donation of over 500 euros must be registered and published. The ELDR (European Liberal Democrat and Reform) Party will get about 800,000 euros per year to run a secretariat, organise meetings, print a manifesto, etc. Currently, these parties are funded by their national member parties and their political groups in the European Parliament, where their secretariats are housed. This will no longer be allowed.

\*\*\*

On Thursday I was in Thessaloniki to host the meeting of Liberal leaders in advance of the European Council (summit) meeting. Sadly, our Finnish prime minister resigned at 6.00pm on Wednesday after only two months in office, caught up in a scandal about whether she lied about how she obtained sensitive government information which she used as ammunition in her election campaign. As one wag put it 'how quaint that a Prime Minister should resign for lying'! She will probably be succeeded by the current Defence minister, but it meant we had only three Liberal Prime Ministers at our press conference. We agreed to back the draft EU constitution drawn up by the Convention on the future of Europe: to call for an end to the national veto in the EU's common foreign and security policy, seeking decision making by super-qualified majority instead (ie. a decision could be taken if supported by countries representing five sixths of the EU's population); and to re-commit ourselves to enlargement. Moreover we called for a political solution to the question of Iran's nuclear programme and the avoidance of "another Iraq".

\*\*\*

UK Lib Dem MEPs welcomed to Brussels this week the "No 2" candidates on each regional list. My running mate Tony Welch played a prominent role in the visit which involved briefings by MEPs, observing a debate in the Chamber and attending a meeting of the ELDR MEPs. We've only a year to go 'til the next EP elections and we need to get people up to speed.

\*\*\*

Constituency engagements this weekend include campaigning in a local by-election in Bridgwater (Saturday morning) and a social event in Thornford in the West Dorset constituency. I also meet Malcolm Hanney, current chair of the South West Regional Assembly and take part in a Radio Devon talk show and the BBC's national Politics programme.

*EU've got mail!*

**Monday 30 June**

For parliaments to follow-up legislation can be hugely important. The European Parliament is studying the operation of the law on freedom of information which I pushed through its first reading as Chairman of the Justice and Home Affairs Committee in November 2001 and which was finally adopted in May 2002. The Regulation on Access to Documents, as it is known, requires the EU institutions to publish an annual report on how the law is working. On the basis of the first such reports from Parliament, Commission and Council, we have discovered that the number of requests for information from the European Commission has more than doubled, though surprisingly it is still small compared to the number of requests for information from Parliament and Council. This may be because, although all three institutions have had to publish a register of all documents, the Commission has not yet done this for its specialised agencies. We will insist that it does. The number of requests for Council and Parliament documents has also risen appreciably. MEPs will now push the institutions to adopt a uniform system for reporting categories of request and reasons for refusal to make documents available, to make assessment easier. We will also ask the Ombudsmen to look at cases where the institutions refuse to make documents available, where there is no clear security reason.

\*\*\*

Headlines this week have been about the reform of the CAP agreed by agriculture ministers. Some progress was made, but far too little. Milk and sugar production, which are sensitive for developing country farmers, were left out of the deal. And though payment to farmers for production of some crops will no longer be linked to the amount they produce, overall farm spending will remain the same. Essentially, France managed to put together a coalition of countries to block reform. It's all very depressing. Unless you are a French farmer.

\*\*\*

Readers may recall that I wrote recently about the proposed MEP statute governing Members' salaries and expenses. I reported that Lib Dem MEPs voted against it because it neither made the expenses regime transparent nor put all MEPs on the same footing. During the recent Council meeting (summit) in Thessaloniki the heads of state and governments also rejected it, which does not surprise me in the least. Sadly, it means we're back to the drawing board.

\*\*\*

Two work experience pupils from Gloucestershire (the Sir William Romney School in Tetbury) shadowed me through everything I did this week except my visit to Rome on Friday. There, I supped with a long spoon when I found myself seated next to Prime Minister Berlusconi at dinner in Cesare Borgia's Villa Madonna. I had been critical of him in my address to the conference of La Margherita, our Lib Dem sister party, earlier in the day and he had clearly read reports of what I said on the newswires, which hardly augured well for conviviality. He ladled on the charm, however, and told me how nobody outside Italy understands what is happening in his country. I had to understand that the judges and the journalists were all hard-line communists and that he was the victim of a vicious campaign of character assassination. He struck me as somebody too close to my mind's image of a mafia 'boss' (including his suit and his after shave lotion) for comfort. And just as seriously for the EU, whose Presidency he assumes next week, he failed to give me or the other group leaders a copy of the programme for his Presidency. Five days before it starts, the document has not yet been written (or at least printed). That scares me.

Back to the constituency Saturday morning for a Christian Aid fundraiser in Taunton and a Yeovil Lib Dem garden party in East Coker. I imagine other constituencies in the vast area I cover might also have events on this weekend, but if so they have not told their MEP about them.

## Friday 04 July

Though some of us had feared it, nobody (except Romano Prodi "I know this man. Why did none of you believe me") actually believed that Silvio Berlusconi would blow it in so spectacular a manner. I'd made a barbed comment to him in Rome last Friday about how we expected the President-in-Office of the Council to behave in a manner fitting with the honour and dignity of the post, because having read some of the fairly shocking things he has said as Prime Minister and having recognised that he is out of his depth in politics I felt it important to leave him in no doubt about his probation.

What so offended MEPs was not just the concentration camp jibe[1], which clearly debased his office, but two other comments aimed at all of us. "Lord forgive you, for you know not what you do" might have been tolerated, since Berlusconi was being barracked at that moment by the extreme left. But "you're just the tourists of democracy" was never going to endear him to us. While the bombastic and somewhat offensive remarks of Martin Schulz MEP were in my view regrettable, Berlusconi should not have risen to the bait. He compounded his difficulties by twice declining to withdraw and then holding a press conference in which he dug himself deeper into the hole.

It has been said 'There's no such thing as history; only biography'. This kind of event is certainly the stuff of politics. It makes the blood course through the veins. It's a huge pity that it is so desperately embarrassing to Italy, the country which more than any other has contributed to European unity.

We have to make the Italian Presidency work. The six months ahead are heavily charged, with an intergovernmental conference to agree the new EU constitution, preparations for ten new countries to join us next year and major reforms in economic and agricultural policy. So Parliament's praesidium (the meeting of political group leaders) decided on Thursday to try to defuse matters. We will raise the implicit lack of respect for Parliament in the next ordinary meeting of Council, Commission and Parliament heads (at the end of August) but otherwise continue as normal. However, I doubt Mr Berlusconi will appear before the European Parliament again during his country's Presidency. And I bet Friday's meeting of the EU member state ambassadors and the next meeting of the Council will be pretty unpleasant for Italy's representatives.

It would not surprise me greatly if the whole affair led to Berlusconi's resignation.

Apart from that we've done some pretty useful things this week. Airline passengers will now have a statutory right to compensation for flights or seats cancelled without 'force majeure' and there will be strict labelling requirements for all GM foods.

[1] *Silvio Berlusconi became the President-in-Office of Council on 01 July. On the occasion of his first speech to Parliament where he outlined the Italian Presidency's work programme for the following six months, he rebutted some heckling by German Socialist MEP Martin Schulz about corruption in Italy by suggesting he play the role of a concentration camp leader in a documentary being filmed at the time in Italy. "I know that in Italy there is a man producing a film on Nazi concentration camps - I shall put you forward for the role of Kapo (guard chosen from among the prisoners) - you would be perfect." Mr Schulz and MEPs in the House demanded a withdrawal of his remarks, but Mr Berslusconi flatly refused to do so. The incident led to a dramatic cooling of diplomatic relations between Italy and Germany. Mr Berlusconi also described MEPs as "the tourists of democracy" who had been brainwashed by left-wing newspapers.*

## Friday 11 July

As I write this on Friday afternoon, the European Parliament has risen for its summer recess. I now have a fortnight of constituency engagements followed by a month's break before we return for our autumn session, 25 August to 18 December. (Some of my holiday will be spent working on a book of speeches and essays which I hope to launch in the autumn).

\*\*\*

This week was not a good one for the Commission. Vice-President Neil Kinnock and Commissioner Pedro Solbes came to Parliament on Wednesday to meet political group leaders and members of the Budgetary Control committee to tell us that the internal audit at Eurostat (the EU's statistics office) has discovered breaches of the financial regulations which are more widespread than previously believed. There is evidence of biased awarding of contracts, double accounting and the issue of fictitious contracts. As a result, all contracts with one company have been suspended, disciplinary proceedings opened against three very senior employees and a 20-person enquiry team sent in to report to the new Director within a month. That the Commission should come to Parliament before announcing this to the press is a good sign, and at least they are being open about it. The action taken recognises how serious it is. Parliament's Budgetary Control Committee was given leave to meet during July and August to oversee progress.

\*\*\*

The Convention on the Future of Europe fared rather better. Their final meeting this week to tidy up Part III of the draft EU Constitution went well. National and Euro MPs in the Convention agreed, on a cross-party basis, on the policy areas in which they believe there should be voting by qualified majority in the European Council and co-decision between Council and Parliament. Whether the Italian Presidency has the diplomatic skills to run a successful intergovernmental conference in the autumn to persuade member-state governments to sign up to it is another question. For Berlusconi to manage to insult both his French and German counterparts in consecutive weeks was quite an achievement![1]

\*\*\*

I spent Monday and Tuesday in Romania, visiting Brasov and Bucharest. Brasov is run by our counterparts the National Liberal Party, whose representatives tell of constant pressure from a government which is using many old KGB tactics and acting as if Romania were a one-party state. In Bucharest I met Prime Minister Nastase (not the former tennis player, though the Romanian mens doubles had won at Wimbledon the previous evening) and told him in no uncertain terms that democratic pluralism is a requirement for EU membership. Bulgaria seems to be making progress towards joining the EU in 2007. Romania is not and may even be slipping backwards.

This weekend I talk to party members in Street (tonight), attend a euro campaign planning meeting tomorrow and host a Somerset Liberal Democrat Summit on Sunday. During next week I'll be in Stroud,

Taunton, Bristol, Bath, Launceston, Muchelney and Lydmarsh (Yeovil).

Happy holidays! I'll write again on 29th August.

[1] *The French government recently criticised Berlusconi for refusing to meet Palestinian Authority Chairman Yasser Arafat. Silvio Berlusconi retorted, "France missed a great opportunity to keep quiet," recalling words used by President Jacques Chirac after the candidate states sided with the US over Iraq (see introductory remarks for 2003).*

## Saturday 29 August

Back to Brussels with a vengeance on August bank holiday Monday to discover that the socialist and christian democrat groups have requested a parliamentary debate on the effects of the summer's heat wave. This kind of thing annoys me. To discuss the general effects of global warming is important, but the EU has no competence for forest fires in Portugal or elderly people dying in suffocatingly hot city centres in France. I was not able to prevent a debate, but I managed to banish it to five o'clock next Monday afternoon: it is unlikely any journalists will be around at that time to hear MEPs plead for special funding for their constituencies.

On a more serious note, we will debate Iraq and what the EU should be doing to press the Americans to seek help. Statements from Council and Commission should testify to a growing belief in the EU that we must be able to intervene in peace-creating and humanitarian tasks and an emerging self-confidence in our ability to do so. Operation Concordia in Macedonia - the first EU military mission - is running well and more will certainly follow. Look out for a substantial increase in the EU budget (currently less than EUR 100 billion) to pay for it.

\*\*\*

My main initiative this week has been to secure the support of colleagues for a call on Commissioner Solbes to resign if the Commission's Task Force (due to report later this month on the problems at Eurostat) confirms the malpractices we were told about late in July. I did so and it did not please the Commission. But I saw Romano Prodi privately in Italy during August and told him that Solbes would have to go. The Commission must be seen to take political responsibility for the goings-on at its statistics office. Solbes' argument to the EP Budgetary Control committee in July - that he should not be held responsible for things he was unaware of - is unacceptable. A memorandum of understanding between Parliament and Commission, drawn up at our insistence after we sacked the Santer commission in 1999, obliges the President of the Commission to heed parliamentary calls for the resignation of Commissioners in circumstances such as these. Prodi will have to sack Solbes to draw a line under this matter. If he does not, Parliament will refuse to grant discharge to the EU budget and this will plunge the Union into a deeper crisis.

I normally find the first week back pretty grim and this one has been no exception. But at least it promises to be a lively autumn term.

**Friday 05 September**

An item I should have reported last week is the recent recommendation by the Electoral Commission that Gibraltar should be added to the SW of England Euro Constituency. Finally, the right of Gibraltarians to vote in European Parliament elections will be secured. The Spanish have of course launched a legal challenge, but it is highly unlikely to succeed. I am already in touch with the Gibraltar Liberal party and shall be proud to represent the people of Gibraltar if I am re-elected next year, though I cannot honestly say I welcome the extra travel which will be involved. Tory MEP Giles Chichester is claiming that because I did not sign his petition I was opposed to having the Rock in the SW constituency. The truth is that the Lib Dem MEPs had an agreement not to get involved in lobbying for the claims of competing constituencies.

\*\*\*

Parliament met in Strasbourg this week and our ELDR Group again distinguished itself as the main campaigner on individual rights. One of our Dutch colleagues, Bob van den Bos, presented his report on human rights in the world on behalf of the foreign affairs committee. And my UK colleague Liz Lynne, for the social affairs committee, presented a report on the rights of disabled people, of whom there are 37 million in the EU and 600 million across the world, almost all victims of discrimination of some kind or other. Liz pointed out how a recent EU employment directive is not yet being implemented where the rights of disabled people are concerned; and called for a specific disability directive. The fact is that access to employment, buildings, public transport, financial support, health care, culture, leisure and sport is often denied to people with disabilities; it should not be.

\*\*\*

Valery Giscard d'Estaing was in Parliament on Wednesday to present his draft Constitution for the EU. On 04 October our heads of state and government will open an intergovernmental conference to receive and discuss it. The Italian presidency of the EU hopes to close the conference before Christmas and sign a new Treaty of Rome. If member states try fundamentally to change the Convention's draft, their hopes will be in vain. Indeed, the EU will be plunged into a long and painful bout of constitutional wrangling.

It was a pleasure to see Giscard in operation. Sixty years of political experience have given him marvellous qualities. As chairman of the Convention he was the right man for the moment. Yet for Liberals in the European Parliament he evokes a bitter memory. From 1989 until 1992 he led our Group. His 26 french MEPs constituted half our number. When he defected to the Conservative/Christian Democratic group, taking his MEPs with him, we were severely weakened. The remark hurled at him by Belgian Liberal MEP Jean Defraigne when Giscard announced his planned move to his Liberal Group colleagues is too precious to be left in the powerful hands of oblivion, so I reproduce it here: "Crapule! Foutez le camp!" I restrained myself from the temptation to repeat it in Wednesday's debate.

Last Saturday I was in Falmouth and Camborne constituency. On Friday 5th I will visit Torbay, Totnes and Tiverton. On Saturday we have a European election campaign team meeting.

*EU've got mail!*

**Friday 12 September**

Three referenda are underway which are all, in their way, important. I was in Estonia on Monday and Latvia on Tuesday campaigning with our Liberal colleagues in each country for a 'Yes' vote in their referenda to ratify plans to join the EU next year. Estonia votes on Sunday, Latvia a week later. My guess is that Estonia will vote roughly 70-30% in favour of joining and Latvia 60-40%; concerns about national sovereignty are much higher in the latter.

The third referendum is in Sweden on Sunday, when they vote on Euro entry. I was campaigning in Stockholm on Wednesday. Three years ago Denmark voted No. Will Sweden follow suit? All the opinion polls were predicting a narrow majority for the 'No' camp, but my sense was that the anti-Euro campaign had peaked too soon and that a 'Yes' outcome was gaining ground. Certainly that was the response I got from passers-by who were surprised and perhaps amused to be addressed in English and therefore more willing to stop and chat.

I left Sweden on a flight to Brussels at almost exactly the moment their foreign minister Anna Lindh was brutally stabbed in a department store. The news reached me when I landed in Brussels. She paid the price of a very high public profile; her face is on posters all over Stockholm urging a 'Yes' vote. I knew Anna moderately well; we worked together during the recent Swedish Presidency of the EU on the EU's freedom of information rules. I sat next to her at one or two official dinners. She is a year younger than me and has two boys about the same age as my kids. She was well liked and respected across party boundaries and tipped to be a future Prime Minister. News reports on Wednesday evening told us the injuries were not life threatening. By Thursday morning she was declared dead. It is an outrage which touches me to the quick.

\*\*\*

My 'dining for democracy' initiative continues apace. On Wednesday I supped with senior staff of the UK's Local Government Association. I told them the LGA should convene a conference involving EU, national and local levels of government to discuss how the UK puts EU laws into practice: far too often we are far too heavy handed.

\*\*\*

On Thursday morning I breakfasted with Pedro Solbes, Economic Affairs Commissioner. Solbes has taken a tough line with France over its likely breach of the EU's Growth and Stability Pact, threatening penalties, and my group has supported him. But he told me it needs only an abstention from Germany and Italy (both in danger of breaching the pact themselves) and one other country - Luxembourg say - in the Council of Ministers for the necessary majority to be lacking. No wonder the Swedes have doubts.

Unusually, I am in Brussels on Friday to chair a meeting of the 45 members of staff employed by the Liberal Group. I used the opportunity to breakfast with Commission President Romano Prodi to discuss the Eurostat affair. My group has led calls for a Commissioner to resign if suspicions of wrongdoing during this Commission's term of office are substantiated. Sadly, it would probably be Pedro Solbes. But I've already had him for breakfast.

### Friday 19 September

Well, I was wrong about Sweden. I thought they'd vote Yes by a small margin, but their No was fairly decisive. Where I'd campaigned in Stockholm it was a close run thing, but all areas apart from the very south of the country had a majority against.

What does it mean? Almost certainly that Europe will develop at two speeds. With a UK referendum now unlikely anytime soon and ten new countries joining the EU next May, the Union will have 12 countries with the euro and 13 without. The eurozone accounts for the lion's share of the EU's economic ballast, but tough reforms are still needed to restore growth. Sweden (and the UK) can expect to see inward investment and their influence over economic policy gradually decline, but the sky will not fall in as long as money markets remain stable.

\*\*\*

On Tuesday night I spoke at the launch of the Friedrich Naumann Foundation's new offices in Brussels. Germany's political foundations (each party has one) are an important arm of citizenship education at home and German and foreign policy abroad. Their overt diplomacy was so evidently more successful than the CIA's covert diplomacy that some years ago the Americans moved to copy them. The UK launched the Westminster Foundation for Democracy, which funds work abroad by our political parties, but their budget is miniscule compared to the Germans or the USA.

It was Germany's Naumann foundation which organised my programme in Cambodia earlier this year. Sam Rainsy, the leader of our liberal sister party in Cambodia (which upped its number of MPs substantially in the recent general election) was in Brussels this week seeking help. Prime Minister Hun Sen is refusing to respect the outcome of the poll and trying to set up a minority government (illegal under their constitution). So I've put down an amendment to the EU budget to stop development aid spending until a legitimate government is formed. Cambodia relies heavily on EU aid. My action is more of a warning than an immediate threat, since the new Cambodian government should be formed this autumn while the new EU budget comes into force only on 01 January.

\*\*\*

A sixth former from Wotton-under-Edge, Rachel Hall, work-shadowed me this week. She saw a Liberal Group hopelessly divided over the EU's proposal for computer software patents but mercifully united on most other issues to be voted on in Strasbourg next week. I console myself in the knowledge that all the political groups are divided over the patenting issue. The Commission proposal might even be thrown out altogether. My main fear is that if approved without amendment it could give Microsoft an even greater monopoly in the market.[1]

\*\*\*

MEPs have been granted a higher profile than ever before on the agenda at Party conference in Brighton next week. They've given me a 15 minute speaking slot on Monday morning. I'm not panicking yet, but I will be on Sunday evening!

[1] *The issue of computer patenting was a controversial one. Small and medium sized enterprises were lobbying heavily to try and restrict the patenting of computer software. Most controversy over this was related to the scope of the legislation. At the time, software was already protected by copyright in all Member States. The controversial question was whether software should also be protected by patent in the European Union, the risk being that copyrights protected too little, and patents risked protecting too much.*

## Friday 26 September

For Parliament, this week has been dominated by Commission President Romano Prodi's appearance before the party group leaders to present reports into the Eurostat affair. This is a pity, since other more important things are happening.

The news that the EU is offering the People's Republic of China the chance to buy in to our Galileo global positioning satellite system disturbs me. The Americans will not allow the PRC a key to their system; we appear to be proposing to, in exchange for help with the costs of developing it. Now Israel and Russia have both expressed interest too. Giving such countries access to vital military hardware does not necessarily make the world a safer place.

This needs the kind of thorough public debate and parliamentary approval which the EU's current treaties do not provide for. And to pretend that 15 separate national parliaments can have any real control over what their governments are up to jointly in secret meetings in Brussels is an illusion.

\*\*\*

The discovery by UN weapons inspectors of further traces of enriched uranium in Iran is even more worrying. The Iranians appear to have concluded that to be respected in our world you need to be armed with weapons of mass destruction. However, I believe that the EU's policy of engagement with Iran will be more productive than the USA's reticence.

\*\*\*

The Eurostat 'hearing' came and went and was much overplayed by the media. The reports Parliament received - one from the Commission's Task Force, one from the Internal Audit Service and one from the anti-fraud office - confirmed what we expected. Thankfully they showed that in other 'arms-length' agencies the financial reform package has been implemented properly.

In Eurostat, most of the problems pre-date 1999 (ie. happened before we brought down Jacques Santer's Commission). Some malpractice continued, however, right up until January 2003 when the new financial arrangements had to be in place. I suspect that the full IAS (Internal Audit Service) report, due at the end of next month, will show continuing problems and find evidence of personal enrichment by officials. In my view, Commissioner Solbes will have to resign, though he was unaware of the practices, was persistently lied to by his own director general and let down by his own private office. The total 'value' of the scandal is probably around EUR 5 million. (Total EU budget EUR 96 bn).

\*\*\*

My week started at Lib Dem party conference, where I was given a fifteen minute speaking slot on Monday morning (*Annex, II*). It will finish on Saturday night when I address the Weston-super-Mare LD dinner after visits around Gloucestershire and the former Avon area.

Next week starts horribly few hours afterwards when I drive to Heathrow on Sunday for visits to Washington DC and Ottawa.

**Friday 03 October**

To understand and to put into context European and global politics I find it very valuable to visit the USA at least once a year. While I'm over there I make the short hop up to Ottawa to keep in touch with Canada's Liberals. So this week, a quiet week in Brussels, I've been in Washington DC (Monday and Tuesday) and in Ottawa (Wed, Thur). Here are a few reflections on my visit.

Washington is still in the grips of the most sectarian, oil-money driven government it has known since WW2. For the first time, however, Bush is on the back foot against a newly resurgent Democratic Party. The spirit of national unity which killed political controversy after the terrorist attacks on the world trade towers and the Pentagon is dissipating. I am told it was the New York Times which broke the consensus rather than any politician. However, Members of Congress and Senate are now openly critical of measures such as the Patriot Act and the Military Tribunals Order, with their huge implications for civil liberties, which were adopted in haste in response to the perceived terrorist threat. The $87 bn cost of the occupation of Iraq is being openly challenged. And the new militaristic culture which the Republicans are attempting to introduce is increasingly questioned. The Republicans are still successfully duffing up the Democrats in California, where Governor Gray Davis may be forced out of office to be replaced by Arnold Schwarzenegger (one can hardly think of anybody whose public image better embodies the nature of today's Republican party); but the Democrats may well win the 2004 Presidential race and we may yet see the USA back on board for multilateral co-operation in responding to the challenges of globalisation.

Canada and the EU see eye to eye on such matters. On everything from the Ottawa Land Mines Convention to the International Criminal Court, from Kyoto to reconstruction of Iraq, Canada is with Europe. Indeed, US-Canada relations are at a low ebb. (Though since 87% of Canada's trade is with the USA they are hugely vulnerable to US pressure.)

EU-Canada relations are currently under thorough review on both sides. A refreshingly honest European Commission communication on the subject states that while there is much mutual good will and few problems in our trade relations, there is in practice relatively little mutual understanding and few attempts to deepen relations. The Commission proposes various ideas to overcome this including greater scientific and technical co-operation and more emphasis on people to people dialogue.

Liberals in the EP will play an important role in shaping this new relationship; upon my election as Leader I made sure that the two important inter-parliamentary delegation chairs that our numbers entitle us to included Canada. (The post is ably filled by my Belgian colleague Willy de Clercq.) As an immediate if modest contribution to deepening relations, I offer the Canadian Liberal party a three-month internship every year with our staffers in the EP. They accept and will try to offer a reciprocal opportunity to one of our researchers.

I spent two days meeting MPs and political researchers in the impressive Scots-gothic buildings on Ottawa's parliament hill. As ever when I visit, I am enchanted by Canada. The impact of Liberals having been in government for most of the last century is a country which is remarkably Liberal. They celebrate and encourage diversity; they actively integrate new arrivals, as opposed to the European social democratic belief that toleration is sufficient; they wage war on poverty, ignorance and prejudice and they emphasise solidarity and collective rights alongside individual rights. They are serious about rehabilitation in their prisons. They are generous in development aid.

Please do not misunderstand me. I do not suggest Canada is a paradise, but I find it to be far more a Liberal society than most European countries.

As I left Ottawa on the flight home to London, results were coming in of a Liberal landslide against the Conservatives in the provincial elections in Ontario. Three cheers for Canada!

**Friday 10 October**

An important delegation from the South West came to Brussels this week to learn about the latest developments in EU regional policy and the benefits for the South West of the forthcoming EU enlargement. They held a series of bilateral meetings with European Commission officials and civil servants working in the UK's Permanent Representation (our 'embassy to the EU'). The region's Brussels office ran a seminar on the implications of enlargement at which I was invited to speak. I felt slightly odd talking to local government representatives about business opportunities in the new member countries, since my words might better have been directed to a business audience; but it's important that all of us involved in politics in the region understand how we can further our commercial interests. The EU is about peace and common security, but it has always had a strong business rationale too.

\*\*\*

This week also saw the launch of a piece of shameless self-promotion in the form of my latest book, Liberal Language. In a selection of my speeches and essays over the last five years, I try to give a flavour of my work and an insight into the workings of the EU. It's a cheap book in two senses: easy to put together, since the work is not new; and damn good value at just £9.50! Of course, some parts of the contents were drafted for me by others and I live in fear of a critic writing "This book is both good and original; sadly, the parts which are good are not original and the parts which are original are not very good." But please judge for yourself.

\*\*\*

One or two people have written to me about an alleged EU attack on our hallmarking system for jewellery. Don't believe what you read in the newspapers! First, this is not a new proposal. It was presented a decade ago and has been stuck in the Council of Ministers for the ten years since. The reason for the current attention to what is, to all intents and purposes, a dormant proposal is that the Italian Presidency of the Union have said they want to revive it. Why? Because Italian jewellers are by far the largest exporters within the EU. Their chances of success are almost zero because our fifteen different national systems are very different and nobody wants to harmonise unless it is on the basis of their particular system.

Eight current member states and nine accession states have compulsory hallmarking systems. Under the single market law (the European Single Act) the Commission is charged with making trade between member states easier and thereby reducing prices. What the Commission proposes is not in fact a single EU hallmark but three different means by which equivalence can be established between different hallmarking systems and between hallmarking and self-regulatory systems of quality control. The proposal does not seek to eliminate hallmarking as we know it. So headlines about 'a seven hundred year old system of British hallmarking being wiped out' are bunkum. But of course those who work in the UK's assay offices, and whose salaries add to the costs which manufacturers and importers must pay and therefore pass on to shoppers, are campaigning hard against it.

\*\*\*

There are so many things I could write about each week, one way of finding out about them is to visit the ELDR Group website (www.eurolib.org) or my website (www.grahamwatsonmep.org). I try to keep these missives brief because I know my readers are all busy with campaigning for liberalism. For my part I will be in Bristol today, in North and West Devon tomorrow and in Ankara, Turkey on Sunday addressing the conference of the ruling Law and Justice Party. It's not my preferred way to pass a Sunday, but we're trying to bring them in to the European Liberal Democrat and Reform family.

## Monday 20 October

Last week was a busy one and saw me in Ankara, Vienna, Vilnius, Brussels, Cologne, Brussels again, London and Newcastle.

On Sunday 12 I attended and addressed the first annual conference of Turkey's law and justice party (AKP) since they came to office less than a year ago. I have addressed crowds of between five and eight thousand people at election rallies in Senegal and in Cambodia, but little did I expect to address nearly 30,000 in Turkey. The conference was held in a football stadium on the outskirts of Ankara. Nearly 15,000 crowded inside and a similar number (perhaps more) followed proceedings from outside on a series of large screens. Talking to so many, especially through an interpreter, can only work if the message is short and sweet.

Mine was. If you get it right, EU Lib Dems will support Turkey's entry to the EU; and since you are doing what Liberal parties did in western Europe a hundred years ago with your package of constitutional and social reforms we want you with our political family. It went down well.

\*\*\*

I flew via Vienna (Sunday night, and a meeting with Liberal friends there) to Vilnius, where I led the delegation leaders from the ELDR Group in meetings with the three Lithuanian parties who are affiliated to us. One has the President, one the foreign minister and one is in opposition but has the mayor of the capital city, Vilnius. We visited the border with the Ukraine and I laid a wreath at the memorial for seven Lithuanian soldiers killed by the Russians during the independence movement in the early 1990s. I was sorry to see that the EU has insisted on a border which resembles too closely the former Soviet border with the West, to deter would-be immigrants. The Ukranian border guards we spoke to told us the EU had paid some of their costs, but much of the burden fell on poverty-ridden Ukraine.

\*\*\*

Back to Brussels Tuesday evening for a conference I am hosting on Wednesday on EU defence policy. Alongside our Lib Dem defence ministers from Luxembourg and Estonia is the Turkish Minister of Defence, Vecdi Gonul, the biggest crowd-puller of the day and doubtless a return favour for my visit there at the weekend. NATO chose Wednesday morning to announce the establishment of its rapid reaction force, and deputy secretaries general Alessandro Minuto Rizzo and Jamie Shea, both speakers at the conference, confirmed that it can co-exist happily with and even complement the EU's planned reaction force provided that they share common planning assumptions. (In other words, don't put anyone in the position of having to choose between supplying fighter aircraft for NATO and tanks for their EU commitment.) The anger expressed by the USA about Blair's agreement to such a scheme at this week's summit seems to me misplaced. NATO is changing in response to developments on both sides of the Atlantic; this does not mean it is disintegrating.

\*\*\*

On Thursday morning I attended the breakfast for ELDR family Prime Ministers hosted by Belgian PM Guy Verhofstadt in advance of that afternoon's European Council (EU summit). We found much common ground on defence related issues and on pan-European infrastructure investments. Late that afternoon, after a busy day of meetings, I was driven to Cologne to address a meeting of the German Free Democrats with Alexander Count Lambsdorff, son of Otto Count Lambsdorff, who will be one of their leading candidates for the elections to the European Parliament next year. Recounting to them something of my week, I was depressed to find so much hostility to possible membership of Turkey in the EU.

\*\*\*

The Spanish have been knocking hard at my door this week to persuade me to help them water down the terms of the European Parliament's enquiry into the sinking of the 'Prestige'. The leader of their MEPs and their foreign minister (a former MEP) both came to see me. I am not prepared to budge. Had their government not handled the affair so badly, I might have more sympathy for their case.

\*\*\*

On Friday I addressed a conference on Taiwan at the School for Oriental and African Studies the University of London and on Saturday the annual conference of the Northern Region Liberal Democrats (in Newcastle). We hope to pick up a seat there next June which we narrowly missed in June 1999.

## Monday 27 October

Parliament was in plenary session in Strasbourg this week. For me, the week had much to do with Senegal.

When we elected Pat Cox as President (speaker) of the House 21 months ago, I moved that we invite Abdoulaye Wade, President of Senegal, as the first African head of state to address Parliament in the current mandate. Since Wade is a Liberal, Cox agreed with alacrity. And this week we had one of the best addresses I've heard in nearly ten years in parliament.

This impressive 77 year old head of state spent thirty years (some of it in jail as a political prisoner) trying to oust Socialist Abdou Diouf before finally succeeding. Since then, Senegal has been one of the best run countries on the continent. Wade's approach is engaging and intuitive. 'Keep your agricultural subsidies if you want to', he told us; 'but since they are against the spirit of the WTO, pay compensation to the countries who suffer'. Not a bad idea for Cancun[1] and at least it would make Europe and the US assess the full cost of policies which may be socially desirable but wreak havoc in our trading relations with poorer countries.

On Thursday I travelled to Dakar, to meet Wade on Friday morning, for the second time in three days, at the Liberal International conference which he hosted this year. I delivered a speech on the conference theme 'Islam and the West'. I argued that the real divide in today's world is between those who believe in a secular state and those who want religious politics: Liberals in both christian and islamic countries are on the same side of that divide.

\*\*\*

In Strasbourg the most important thing we did this week was to vote the EU's budget (first reading) for 2004. The Liberal group normally gets the chance to nominate the rapporteur (pilot) for the budget once in every five year term, and this year it was the turn of my (Dutch) colleague Jan Mulder. He has done a good job, finding money in a difficult budgetary year to prioritise Liberal ideas, e.g. to fund small business start-ups in the western Balkans and to give more resources to the new international criminal court, set up under UN auspices to try people guilty of crimes against humanity.

Our alliance with the christian democrats paid dividends this week too. I was able to persuade them to back the establishment of a temporary committee on maritime safety (in the wake of the Prestige, Erika and other disasters) and to agree to launch a report into the threats to freedom of expression posed by near-monopoly ownership of the media, especially in Italy. Since they have both the Spanish Partido Popular and Berlusconi's Forza Italia within their group, this was not easy for them. But by brokering with the left wing parties texts to which the right could agree, we managed to secure a united approach and one on which consensus may be built.

I'm taking my kids on a few days holiday next week so may not report.

[1] *The fifth Ministerial Conference of the World Trade Organisation was to take place in Cancun, Mexico at the beginning of September.*

## Monday 10 November

The 'executive committee' of my group of MEPs is called the 'Bureau'. It consists of the leader of each national political party represented in the ELDR group. It normally meets once a month to discuss staffing and resource use. But it has a more strategic role in the prelude to, and the immediate aftermath of, a European election campaign.

That is why we spent Monday afternoon and evening and Tuesday morning in Luxembourg at a strategy session. We agreed the broad outlines of plans for next June's euro election, including the ELDR party conference in Amsterdam next week and a campaign rally in Brussels in late March or early April 2004. They approved my proposal to ask our MEPs on each committee to do some 'blue-skies' thinking about what European Liberal Democrat priorities would be for legislation in our next five year mandate. We can then use these ideas to elicit commitments from the Liberal Commissioners in the next European Commission (we expect to have 5 or 6 Commissioners from the Liberal family). And they agreed that we should put forward a candidate from the Liberal family for the Presidency of the European Commission, not least since the other parties will do so. In such ways is a pan-European democracy beginning to take shape.

\*\*\*

The main item of business at our two day plenary session in Brussels this week was the presentation by the Commission of its reports on progress by the EU candidate countries towards joining the Union. This is an annual report, charting their progress towards fulfilling the criteria for membership of the EU. For the ten countries due to join us on 01 May next year the Commission reported a total of fewer than forty 'serious concerns', out of 140 policy areas in each state. Almost all the concerns are to do with food safety and public health or with the quality of public administration. Though Poland had its wrist slapped more than any other country, the Commission is confident they will all make the grade by 01 May 2004.

Yet much energy has been invested in recent days in relations with two other countries, Russia and China. There was an EU-China summit in Beijing last week and an EU-Russia summit in Rome this week.

In my view we are proceeding too fast with China. Dialogue, yes; help with the transition to democracy, yes; but sale of military hardware, no. The decision to involve China in the development of Galileo, the EU's nascent global-positioning-by-satellite system, is an ethical disgrace and a political blunder and will harm our relations with the USA.

As for Russia, co-operation will cover everything but institutions. In other words we want their launch capacity to put our satellites into space and are prepared to co-operate in many areas, but we will not offer the prospect of membership of the EU. The issue of Russia's apparent persecution of the private Yukos oil company (because they supported political parties opposed to Putin) was not even raised. It should have been. And if anybody other than Silvio Berlusconi had been presiding the summit, it would have been.

\*\*\*

I was pleased to welcome to Brussels a small group of visitors from Mid Dorset and North Poole constituency, a local government association delegation led by Councillor Chris Clarke of Wells, fellow euro candidate Tony Welch and Theodor Stolojan, the leader of Romania's

National Liberal party, the country's main opposition party. This morning (Friday) I addressed the Swedish Liberals' annual conference and this evening I shall introduce my colleague Nick Clegg MEP, guest speaker at Somerton and Frome constituency's annual dinner.

Weekend commitments include campaigning in local by elections in Swindon (Sat am) and Tewkesbury (Sat pm) and taking my family to a Weston-super-Mare Lib Dem firework night in Shipham.

Happy campaigning.

**Monday 17 November**

A sign that the UK is beginning to take its MEPs seriously was our invitation to join MPs at a Buckingham Palace reception on Monday. I imagined we would simply get a handshake in a receiving line and that would be it, but to Her Majesty's credit she moved around among us and chatted to each huddle in turn. When I asked whether she shared the views attributed to her in the press - that the new EU Constitution poses a threat to the royal family - she rolled up her eyes in disbelief. But I would be hard pushed to conclude from our brief conversation that she is a great fan of the EU.

\*\*\*

I've won my battle for a debate with Council and Commission on the EU citizens detained at Guantanamo Bay. The Council will make a statement at our December session. Next week in Strasbourg we get statements on the EU-Russia summit (another chance to lambast Silvio Berlusconi and to express anger at the failure to mention Chechnya in the meeting's communiqué)[1] and the EU-Canada summit, again at my request because I want to raise the profile of EU-Canada relations.

The main debate next week, however, will be on the Commission's work programme for 2004. This innocuous sounding debate is our equivalent of Westminster's debate on the Queen's speech. Prominent among the

Commission's proposals is a Directive on Gender Discrimination, which will have my strong support. It will cover gender discrimination wherever it occurs, but in the UK press it has featured only as a threat to the lower driving insurance premiums paid by women (a story planted by the insurance companies, of course, who could be obliged to stop discriminating against male drivers). As Commissioner Diamantopoulou points out, however, it's not the chromosome which determines driving ability.

\*\*\*

Much of my week was spent in Amsterdam at the ELDR party congress, where we adopted our manifesto for next year's European elections. It is recommended reading for insomniacs. For that reason among others, we'll organise a rally in Brussels in April/May to launch the campaign formally and boil down the manifesto to five key policies on one A4 folded glossy leaflet.

UK Libdems were well represented at the conference, our delegation being led by the able Sharon Bowles who I expect to join us as a new MEP next June (South East England constituency).

I spelled out in my speech to the Congress some of the achievements of ELDR MEPs, i.e the votes where our voting decision determined policy (*Appendix, III*).

Tomorrow I'll be at the Western Counties Lib Dem conference in Bath and at the European Movement AGM in Reading and on Sunday evening and Monday at the CBI conference in Birmingham before a speaking engagement in Frankfurt and a late night drive to Strasbourg.

[1] *Despite demands from MEPs across the party divide, Mr Berslusconi, as President-in-Office, did not bring up the question of Russian human rights records over Chechyna at the EU-Russia summit. Indeed he seemed to defend Russia's actions, a significant move away from previous EU policy on Russia. He later said that newspaper reports had distorted his words.*

*EU've got mail!*

**Friday 21 November**

A practical example of how the EU helps us is the Comenius scheme. Schools can benefit from the presence of a classroom assistant from another EU country at little or no cost. They can help out as language or other assistants and are funded from the EU budget. Details of the scheme can be found at www.socrates-uk.net/comenius.

\*\*\*

The main business on our agenda this week was the announcement of the European Commission's 2004 work programme. It contained little to surprise us, so the debate was overshadowed by an attack from the right wing against Commission President Romano Prodi 'for engaging inappropriately in Italian domestic politics'. There is a battle royal going on in Italy between the right, led by Prime Minister Silvio Berlusconi (currently the holder of the EU Council presidency) and the left, led by Prodi (from Brussels). Both men run the risk of allowing their domestic interests to run counter to the neutrality implicit in their EU roles and are sailing pretty close to the wind. In my view we should be able to expect greater self restraint. But all Commission presidents have engaged to some extent in national politics during their time in Brussels; in the case of the late lamented Roy Jenkins, he spent much of his time at the Commission planning the launch of the SDP. It's perhaps naive to believe that people in that position, who all have a political past, may not also have a political future.

\*\*\*

The most important policy issues for MEPs this week were seaports and biotechnology. On the former, Parliament voted (albeit narrowly) to reject at second reading the Port Services Directive, which would have opened up the market in provision of services such as docking and un/loading to inbound and outbound ships. This was a serious defeat of a market liberalisation law which has been five years in the making. I regret it; but at least my troops - bar one - all voted in favour. We will never develop a more competitive economy until we can win these battles!

As for biotechnology, we gave the green light to the funding of embryonic and stem cell research from the EU budget. This will help develop new ways of preventing or providing therapy for neurological and neuromuscular illnesses like Alzheimer's and Parkinson's. We made it clear that such research could not take place in countries where national legislation forbids it, but it will certainly help to strengthen the EU's biotech sector.

\*\*\*

Thursday and Friday see a conference in Strasbourg (where we've been this week) on how to stop the spread of weapons of mass destruction. Of 100 sites in 40 countries where weapons grade nuclear materials are stored, between 20 and 25 are considered to be unsafe (i.e. vulnerable to theft). The G8 has agreed to provide the International Atomic Energy Authority with a fund of US$ 20 bn over ten years to make them safe; $10bn will come from the USA and $10bn from Europe, Russia and Japan combined. I think we will need to argue for a specific budget line for non-proliferation in the Union's budget for the Common Foreign and Security Policy. We've recently established in the Council of Ministers a security centre staffed by intelligence agents from different EU member states, but much more co-operation is needed. Rumours earlier this year that a ten kilotonne nuclear weapon had been smuggled into New York by terrorists had American policy makers seriously on edge for over a week. The tragic bombings in Istanbul testify to the ever present threat[1]. Which of Europe's major cities is not vulnerable?

\*\*\*

I spoke to a German Free Democrat rally in Schwalbach near Frankfurt on Monday night. This time no questions about Turkey's membership of the EU, thank heavens, though they notably failed to applaud when I reached that part of my speech. I felt a bit like Blair must have felt at the CBI conference on Monday - the audience was not convinced (though in Blair's case because he was too hesitant on the development of the EU!)[2]

Tomorrow (Friday) I'll be in Ilfracombe in the morning, campaigning in a county council by-election, and speaking later at a Tewkesbury

*EU've got mail!*

constituency pizza and politics evening. On Saturday I address the AGMs of the Devon and Cornwall region and West Dorset and East Devon constituencies. If you're a reader of these missives and attending one of these events, please come up and let me know what you think of them.

[1] *A double suicide bomb attack in Istanbul this week left at least 27 dead and over 400 injured. The bombs exploded at the UK consulate and HSBC Bank headquarters.*

[2] *The accession of Turkey to the EU is a controversial one in Germany, not least due to the number of Turkish immigrants Germany is home to.*

**Monday 01 December**

The European Union's boast (in March 2000) that it will have by 2010 'the most competitive, dynamic, knowledge based economy in the world' looks pretty threadbare this week. Not only do the latest economic growth statistics show that the USA's economy grew four times as fast as Europe's in the third quarter of this year, but three developments this week show how we are failing to get our act together.

The first is the declaration by the UK and Germany that they will not compromise on their demands at the intergovernmental conference. Both countries recognise that the EU needs more majority voting if it is to complete the EU single market; each has also said it will not accept majority voting on certain areas of policy. If all countries go into next month's meeting with that attitude, there will be no agreement. Unanimity will be required for almost everything, which means that any country of the 25 will be able to block any decision which the other 24 deem necessary. Britain's veto over tax policy is Greece's veto over reform of the agricultural subsidies; Germany's veto over competition policy is Estonia's veto over something else. It adds up to gridlock in decision-making.

The second is the fiasco over the EU's 'Growth and Stability Pact'. At Germany's insistence, this agreement laid down (in 1996) rules for economic policy to ensure that the euro would be as strong as the

German Mark (because of the Germany's trauma of high inflation after the war). Countries adopting the euro agreed to cut their public debt and keep their annual deficit to less than 3% of GDP. (I sat on Parliament's economic and monetary affairs committee at the time and I remember saying that this was daft, reflecting short term Friedmanite economic fashion rather than a serious long term approach to currency management.) Countries like the Netherlands have had to introduce painful measures to stick to these disciplines. Germany and France have failed to do so and have used strong-arm tactics this week to avoid the penalties for non-compliance. The message it sends is this: small countries have to abide by the rules; big countries don't. This psychology is deeply damaging to the EU and will have broader repercussions. Probably the only reason that the euro has not fallen on financial markets is that Japan and the USA have larger deficits (5% and 8% respectively, if my memory serves me right).

The third setback has been the deal on EU legislation on company takeovers. Member states have pushed through a measure, against the advice of the European Commission, which will allow them the discretion to protect their companies from foreign takeover bids through the use of 'poison pills' which make such takeovers prohibitively expensive. Competitiveness suffers.

\*\*\*

Much of the European Parliament's work is in the field of human rights. Liberals have recently championed the causes of the Ivory Coast (where President Gbagbo is riding roughshod over the peace agreement sponsored earlier this year by France, on behalf of the EU) and of the Seychelles, where the government has taken to bumping off its opponents and is now openly sanctioning money laundering and the trade in drugs and small arms.

My group has secured a statement from the European Council and a debate next week in Brussels on the former. The EU can do more to put pressure on Gbagbo to introduce democratic reforms in the Ivory Coast and to drop his policy of 'Ivority' which discriminates against many sections of a heterogeneous population. The EU can act too to force President Albert Rene of the Seychelles to restore the rule of law; but to my horror, Commissioner Nielson (in charge of development policy) and MEP Glenys Kinnock, a leading member of the EP's development co-operation committee, have sided with Rene because his party is a member of the Socialist International. They accuse Liberals of fomenting the issue for party political reasons, because the Seychelles opposition is part of the Liberal International. So much for objectivity!

\*\*\*

I frequently ask Commission officials to come and see me to brief me on particular issues or to help with constituents' difficulties. It is not often they ask to come and see me. This week, the head of unit responsible for China, Taiwan and Hong Kong did. His pretext was that he took up his current post only in February and recognised my interest in the area. The sub-text was that I have rattled Commissioner Patten's cage with my criticisms of his China strategy, especially when I attacked him for selling military hardware (in the form of our nascent Galileo GPS system) to the People's Republic of China. I learned that the Commission has no fewer than 100 people from different departments working on relations with China. The Chinese are very interested in developing closer links with the EU. We have senior PRC visitors almost every week now (and they are much more 'westernised' than they used to be) and they want us to lift the embargo on selling them arms. I fear that some EU member states are planning to agree to this. Yet to do so would be to risk engaging in competition with the USA in a Dutch auction on human rights.

For all its 'modernisation', the PRC is the world's only significant remaining vile communist dictatorship, with a human rights record which (according to Amnesty International) is currently getting worse rather than better. The EU should be much more circumspect in its dealings with China. We will need to organise parliamentary opposition to any change in policy.

**Friday 05 December**

My recent report on the freeing up of EU funds for stem cell research[1] was premature, I'm afraid. The proposal from the Commission and Parliament was blocked in the European Council by member state governments unwilling to sanction it. I suspect we are unlikely to see progress under the Irish Presidency in the first half of next year, so it may have to wait until the Netherlands Presidency next autumn.

The most important policy development in Parliament this week was the agreement on new rules for public procurement. Currently, any government tender over a certain value must be put out to competition across the EU. But the rules governing this come from four separate directives. Following two readings in Parliament and Council of a European Commission proposal for simpler rules, a 'conciliation committee' met to hammer out a compromise. These committees consist of one representative per member state and an equal number of representatives of the EP. They meet into the wee small hours, over a number of days if necessary, until agreement is reached on contentious matters. The only unresolved problem in this case was the criteria for awarding public contracts. MEPs won the right for factors other than price, e.g. environmental considerations, to be taken into account in the awarding of contracts, though only within clearly defined rules. Parliament and Council must each now vote to approve the agreement. We will. It is very rare for such an agreement then to be defeated in a vote in either institution, which would not only prevent it becoming law but would send the whole matter right back to the drawing board.

\*\*\*

On Thursday I met Commission officials to try to get more funding for the European Voluntary Service scheme in Somerset. Lib Dem run Somerset County Council is a recognised pioneer of this scheme, whereby the county can send disadvantaged youngsters, including those with learning difficulties or physical disabilities, to spend three months living and working with others of different nationalities in another EU member state; and also agrees to host similar youngsters from other

*EU've got mail!*

member states. It is as a host that Somerset excels, with projects in Yeovil, Taunton, Highbridge and Minehead. But government cuts mean that social services will be restricted to tasks required by statute and this scheme is likely to be discontinued, which would be a great pity. The Commission tells me there is no way they can provide more, so I'll be knocking at the door of the British Council (the national organiser of the scheme) next. With local government in the UK so utterly dependent on national government for funding we fare very poorly compared to other countries in initiatives such as these; and the rare jewels such as this scheme in Somerset are hugely vulnerable.

\*\*\*

My week began with a visit to Geneva, where I led an official delegation of Parliament (cross party) to the launch of the Geneva Initiative for Middle East peace. When governments cannot or will not make peace, citizens' action can sometimes be a powerful tool (as the peace women in Northern Ireland showed). Civil society in Israel and Palestine, led by Yossi Beilin and Yasser Abed Rabbo respectively, is showing the way forward. The Swiss government has supported their work. We were there to add our support.

I then flew overnight to Moscow to campaign on Tuesday in support of Grigory Yavlinski's Yabloko (Apple Tree) party. Putin has effectively killed any independence in the judiciary, he has closed down independent TV, he is silencing political opposition by jailing those who fund opposition parties (such as Mikhail Khodorkovsky[2]) and may well try to rig Sunday's general election ballot to deprive Yavlinski's party, which is the only independent opposition, of seats in the Duma (parliament). I attended a demonstration against a hike in student fees organised by Yabloko students, gave an interview to Radio Liberty in support of Yabloko and ran a press conference jointly with Grigory Yavlinski to express support from EU Liberals. I hope that it was helpful to him, even if only in a small way. He needs it.

Tomorrow (Friday) I've a full day of constituency engagements including a talk to pupils at Filton High School and the Bristol NW constituency dinner.

[1] See letter of 21 November.

[2] Mr Khodorkovsky, former head of oil giant Yukos was jailed on allegations of tax evasion and fraud. He was also a financial supporter of three opposition parties, including Yabloko.

**Friday 12 December**

While the focus of this week in Brussels has been on this weekend's intergovernmental conference (IGC), a breakthrough has been made in another area which will have a more immediate impact on the lives of Europe's citizens. In a conciliation committee after second reading the EP and the member states have hammered out a deal on a 'single European sky'. Currently there are fifteen separate national air traffic control systems and very little airspace to fly in, most of it being reserved for military use (though we're enjoying our longest unbroken period of peace on record!). The new agreement is a first step in a new policy which will make more airspace available for commercial traffic, will take air traffic control from the age of the corner shop to the era of the supermarket and will cut delays and therefore the huge air pollution involved in 'stacking' aircraft over airports.

\*\*\*

Liberal Democrat fears that toppling Saddam Hussein before restoring law and order and good governance in Afghanistan would lead to overstretching our resources are proving justified. Over the last ten months, local warlords in Afghanistan have started killing aid workers again and poppy cultivation has risen to a level 30 times higher than when the Taliban regime was ousted two years ago. Figures from the US government show that 61,000 hectares were used for opium poppy cultivation this year compared to 30,700 last year and fewer than 1,700 the year before.

\*\*\*

My efforts in my first two years of ELDR Group leadership paid off handsomely today (Thursday) when both the Bulgarian and the Turkish prime ministers attended the Lib Dem prime ministers' gathering which I convene ahead of the EU summit. The Bulgarian PM's party was accepted into the ELDR party at our Congress in Amsterdam last month; I expect the Turkish Law and Justice party to apply for observer member status before too long. It means we now have three Liberal PMs in the EU and three in the candidate countries. It also means the international press take us far more seriously; their numbers at our press conference and family photo today were certainly higher than normal.

We were able to get our summit participants to commit themselves to pressing for more majority voting in the Council of Ministers, which is what the EU needs to overcome the current gridlock in decision-making which results from individual national vetoes; and to send a message to Blair, Schroeder, Chirac and Aznar that they need to raise their game, because if they each go into this weekend's talks with their 'red lines' there will be no agreement. If, after 40 years of EU co-operation, we do not trust each other enough to agree to majority voting in most policy areas, why do we have the EU? (In any case it would be a qualified majority, with decisions needing not just a majority of countries but a majority of countries representing also a majority of the EU's population.)

I await the outcome of this summit with interest. I'm not sure our national leaders have the vision and the courage to reach agreement. Yet pessimism of the intellect should go together with optimism of the will, and blame for any failure this weekend cannot be laid at the feet of the EU's Liberal Democrat and Reform family.

While the summiteers are hard at work tomorrow (Friday) I shall be talking to pupils at St Luke's school in Exeter, attending a Lib Dem Team for Somerset meeting in Yeovil and addressing a Lib Dem meeting in Fairford in Gloucestershire. On Saturday I'll be trying to clear up the constituency casework generated by my 4.9 million constituents in time for Christmas. Fortunately not all of them write to me, but this week I will sign my 50,000th letter to a constituent since my election nine and a half years ago.

## Monday 22 December

The EU institutions heaved a massive collective sigh of relief this week as Silvio Berlusconi put in his final appearance as President-in-Office of the EU Council of Ministers. Nobody is sorry to see him go. His Presidency was poorly prepared and badly managed. He offended our allies in Canada and India by cancelling the summit meetings planned with them and cosied up to the Russians and Chinese as if they shared our values.

Despite the poor progress record on policy dossiers currently on the EU's agenda (only five were completed under his stewardship) he had the gall to treat MEPs to a 40 minute eulogy of his own Presidency, which he described as 'the most glorious in recent years'. Somebody had to put him right. It fell to me to do so since the first speaker to reply to the debate, EPP leader Hans-Gert Poettering, has Berlusconi's MEPs in his parliamentary group and the second, Socialist leader Enrique Baron, cannot say boo to a goose. I was fairly harsh and not terribly polite and received more applause than for any speech I've made since becoming leader. I could not have hoped for a better Christmas present from my colleagues (*Appendix, IV*).

\*\*\*

At the joint initiative of Lib Dems and the Greens the EP debated and passed a resolution this week on the EU embargo on arms sales to China. Hidden away in paragraph 71 of the Statement (Presidency Conclusions, these statements are called) from last weekend's EU summit was a request from our heads of state and government to their foreign ministers to review this embargo. To my satisfaction, all political parties in the House except the extreme left voted a strongly worded resolution insisting the embargo must stay. Though Parliament currently has no formal powers to stop arms sales it will be hard in practice for the foreign ministers to ignore a resolution adopted with such a huge majority.

\*\*\*

*EU've got mail!*

Surprising and pleasing progress was made this week on the matter of MEPs' expenses. Parliament was finally able to adopt a text insisting that travel and other expenses be reimbursed to members on the basis of the cost of the ticket rather than on distance travelled. Since the advent of low cost airlines, MEPs flying out of major airports like London, Rome and Athens have been able to make a hefty profit on their travel. At the same time, we urged that all MEPs be paid a common salary with effect from next July (when the new parliament takes office), which means a pay cut for the Germans and Italians and substantial improvement for the Spanish and Portuguese. UK MEPs will also be better paid. Disgracefully, the British Tories refused to vote for reform and just sat on their hands.

\*\*\*

My week finished in Dublin, where all the party leaders from the EP were invited to meet Taoiseach Bertie Ahern and his foreign secretary and EU affairs minister to discuss their EU Presidency, which starts on 01 January. They are much better prepared than the Italians and - though they are not optimistic - will try to broker agreement on the new EU Constitution on which talks at the Brussels summit collapsed. Small countries often make good Presidencies; and the charm of the Irish will certainly help.

No constituency engagements this weekend, because 20 Watsons are descending on us for the annual pre-Christmas gathering of the clan. Parliament rises today, so I wish all my readers a happy Christmas and whatever they seek from 2004. My constituency office will be closed 24-28 December and 01-02 January but otherwise open. I will write again on 09 January, the end of our first week back.

Graham and Charles Kennedy at the
Autumn Liberal Democrat Conference in Brighton.
September 2003

Campaigning to save local post offices,
with Liberal Democrat PPC for Bournemouth, Andrew Garrett.
October 2003

*Family photo at the ELDR Leaders' summit, Brussels December 2003*
Front row, from L to R: German FDP floor leader Wolfgang Gerhardt, Bulgarian Prime Minister Simeon Saxe-Coburg-Gotha, ELDR Party President Werner Hoyer, ELDR Group Leader Graham Watson, Belgian Prime Minister Guy Verhofstadt, European Parliament President Pat Cox, Danish Prime Minister Anders Fogh Rasmussen, Finnish Prime Minister Matti Vanhanen.

Graham meeting UN Secretary General Kofi Annan, January 2004. Mr Annan received Parliament's Sakharov Prize for human rights on behalf of the UN and in memory of UN staff killed in Baghdad in 2003.

Discussing Cambodian affairs with Prince Norodom Ranariddh, President of the Cambodian National Assembly, and Sam Rainsy, MP & Vice-President of the Democratic Alliance.
February 2004

*Looking serious at the ELDR Leaders' summit, Brussels Spring 2004*
From L to R: Belgian Prime Minister Guy Verhofstadt, European Commission President Romano Prodi, Turkish Prime Minister Recep Tayyip Erdogan, ELDR Group Leader Graham Watson.

*A new European political party formation?*
UDF leader Francois Bayrou, European Commission President
Romano Prodi and Graham Watson.
Brussels 03 March 2004

Graham with wife Rita and children Frederica and Gregory.
November 2003

# 2004

*The start of 2004 was overshadowed by the failure of member states to agree on the EU Constitution at the European Council meeting in Brussels in December 2003. While a stalemate had been reached over voting rights in the Council (Spain and Poland were unmoving in their resolve to stick to the agreements reached at Nice in 2000 which would give them more voting powers than the Constitution draft proposed), the Irish government which took over the helm in January made a conscious effort to relaunch the Intergovernmental Conference in order to agree a final Constitution before the end of its presidency. The fall of the Popular Party government in Spain in March also opened a window of opportunity for further negotiations.*

*Parliament was still talking in 2004 about the downfall of the growth and stability pact, which member states had resolutely ignored in November 2003 rather than face fines for breach of the rules. And EU enlargement remained high on the agenda, as 01 May 2004 drew ever closer. The ten applicant states each nominated a Commissioner, who would shadow a current Commissioner until the end of the mandate in October. Parliament vetted these choices during April, and held a formal vote during the last parliamentary session in May.*

*Terrorism returned to the top of the EU agenda in March with the tragic loss of life in Madrid following a ten-bombed attack on commuter trains at rush hour on 11 March. Member states which had not yet implemented legislation following the terrorist attacks in New York and Washington on 11 September were named and shamed, and EU Justice Ministers decided to appoint an anti-terrorism co-ordinator to oversee the EU's response to the threat of terrorism.*

*At the forefront of the minds of MEPs was the next round of European elections, to take place between 10-13 June.*

*EU presidencies in 2004 were held by Ireland and the Netherlands.*

## Friday 09 January

The mouse is about to roar. Commissioner Solbes, in charge of monetary policy, will seek to persuade his colleagues in the European Commission - on the basis of clear legal advice - to take the Member States to court over November's decision by the EU's finance ministers to exempt France and Germany from the rules of the growth and stability pact.

He has a point. The European Commission is legally obliged to uphold EU law. It is, indeed, the 'guardian of the EU treaties', as the Treaty of Rome puts it. When Member States themselves decide to ride roughshod over the Treaties they have signed, the Commission has no choice but to act. And Pedro Solbes is a man of great tenacity and determination.

A ruling by the European Court of Justice in the Commission's favour would not actually change very much, but it would at least force member states formally to re-write the rules which say that a eurozone country's budget deficit must not exceed 3% for more than three consecutive years. And it would show the Council of Ministers that they are not free to make up new rules as they go along. I hope the Commission agrees to Solbes' proposal.

Respect for the rules of the growth and stability pact might also help Tony Blair to get the UK into the euro by 2007, which he says he wants. His constituency is not far from Sunderland, where Nissan have again said that they will switch investment to the continent - with all the UK job losses this implies - unless Britain adopts the common currency. Euro membership is not the only factor which influences investment decisions, but the UK's falling share of the North American and Asian investment coming into the EU is clearly worrying Downing Street. With little manufacturing of our own we rely more heavily than other countries on such investment.

\*\*\*

The European Parliament's new term got off to a hair-raising start with three MEPs receiving letter bombs. Fortunately they were only incendiary devices and nobody was injured. My UK Labour colleague

Gary Titley received his at his constituency office in Manchester; I have put my staff on the alert. Much more worrying, however, is that the two which were sent to Parliament's Brussels offices were not picked up in the scanning machines; almost certainly because the employees of Group 4 Falck security were not paying attention while scanning the mail. The European Parliament may well sue the company for breach of contract.

The staff member who opened one of the booby-trapped packages was an eighteen year old law student on the first day of her work experience in the office of the leader of the European People's Party (christian democrats). We are extremely lucky to have received a warning to step up our security procedures without anyone being seriously hurt.

\*\*\*

Labour voters are more pro-European than Liberal Democrats - it's official. A poll for The Times asked how people would define their attitudes to the EU on a scale of one to ten, from the very sceptical to the very positive. The average score was 4.58, which means that voters generally are slightly but not very sceptical. The Tories average was 3.94 (more sceptical), ours was 4.82 (slightly more pro-EU than the average but still sceptical on balance), while Labour voters averaged 5.2. Am I in the wrong party? On reflection, no. But perhaps I have to work harder to persuade fellow Lib Dems of the case for the EU. A Happy New Year to you!

## Friday 16 January

The European Commission this week published its draft Directive on Services. The single market, designed to make the EU more competitive by opening up cross-border trade, has worked wonders for the trade in goods. But more wealth is created now in the provision of services than in the production of goods and there are barriers a-plenty when it comes to offering services across national borders. Liberal Democrats have welcomed this long-overdue proposal for a framework directive, which will set the overall policy framework for specific sectoral directives to follow in due course.

This is not to be confused with a call from the left of the House for a Directive on Services of General Interest. The socialists and former communists argued that the Commission should bring forward a directive laying down rules covering water, energy, telecoms, postal services etc. Their aim was clearly to prevent governments introducing any more private competition into such areas. We defeated the move by a reasonable majority, since in the end a good number of so-called socialists voted with us, including most of the UK Labour MEPs.

\*\*\*

The main set-piece debate of our week in Strasbourg was the formal presentation to Parliament by Taoiseach Bertie Ahern of the Irish Presidency's programme. In my view it's a good one, modest in its ambitions but serious in its intent, and on behalf on my colleagues I gave it a general welcome. Ireland wants a particular focus on Africa with regard to increasing development aid, doing more to fight Aids and writing off debt.

Perhaps the point which stimulated most debate, however, was the Taoiseach's statement last week that the next President of the Commission, who will be nominated under the Irish Presidency, need not necessarily be a serving or former prime minister. (Neither Jenkins nor Delors was, though both Santer and Prodi were.) Some interpreted this as opening the door for Pat Cox, our ELDR President of Parliament, who is highly regarded and might give Ireland its first chance to have an Irishman at the head of the EU's executive. In any case it brought a response this week from Hans-Gert Poettering, leader of the right wing European People's party, who said that if they were the biggest party after the election (very likely) they would expect the President of the Commission to be chosen from their ranks. The battle to succeed Prodi is on.

\*\*\*

A new word entered my vocabulary this week: ochlocracy. I learned from German christian democrat politician Wolfgang Schauble, via the pages of the Financial Times, that it was coined by Plato to describe a democracy in which there is little justice because the majority imposes its will unfairly on the minority (J S Mill called it 'the tyranny of the majority'). Schauble argues convincingly that the row over the failure to apply the rules of the growth and stability pact to France and Germany shows that the bigger countries in the EU seek adherence to democracy, where they can use their voting power to throw their weight around, while smaller countries seek the rule of law, which protects minority interests. This, he argues, is the crisis at the heart of the EU today. Indeed it is true that the current rifts are caused not by countries defending what they see as their national interests, but by the manner in which they try to get their way.

The Watson prize for chutzpah goes this week to plucky Brazil. Brazil now photographs and fingerprints every U.S. citizen visiting the country, on the principle of reciprocity![1]

[1] *In a move to step up the fight against terrorism, the US introduced strict security measures at its airports and sea ports in January. All those entering the US with a valid visa would have fingerprints taken and digital photos scrutinised. This did not apply to tourist visas from Europe, Japan or Australia, but all those with work visas were put through the additional measures, together with those with tourist visas from other parts of the world. In an act of retaliation, Brazil decided to impose the same measures on all US citizens entering the country.*

**Friday 23 January**

Two Westminster MPs from the South West came to Brussels this week. Brian Cotter, who I had breakfast with on Tuesday, came with colleagues from the LibDem House of Commons DTI team to talk to Commission, Council and Parliament representatives about issues currently on their agenda. And Richard Younger-Ross came for talks with Commission officials about the problems of the shellfish industry in West Country rivers. I joined him and a representative of the Shellfish Association to protest about the UK's interpretation of the relevant Directive. Since most legislation adopted at Westminster now originates in Brussels such visits are increasingly common. Hardly a week goes by without one or other of our Westminster colleagues coming to Brussels and it is always good to see them.

\*\*\*

On Wednesday the Commission presented to Parliament its recommendations to member states for action to be taken at the March European Council meeting of national leaders. These March meetings are now in their fourth year and are intended to allow governments to review progress on 'the Lisbon agenda', i.e. their plan to give the EU the most competitive, dynamic, knowledge based economy in the world by 2010. As I said in the ensuing debate, progress has been painfully slow. For all their grand words, our national leaders do not have the commitment or the discipline to make the difficult reforms which are necessary. Moreover, they sometimes conspire to defend their perceived national interests in a way that destroys EU progress. To give one example: Britain agreed to join Germany in blocking the Takeovers Directive in exchange for German support for Blair's wish to block the Working Time Directive. Yet unless we have a dynamic economy with at least minimum protection for our workforce we will enjoy neither economic success nor social cohesion. The reason why America's growth rate was four times the EU's in the third quarter of last year is that they invest in research and education, they have integrated capital markets and few barriers to freedom of movement of goods, people, services or capital. We have a long way still to go in this regard.

We also need to commit the cash to invest in infrastructure. Hence the Commission's proposal that from 2006 onwards the EU budget should rise from 1.17% of GNI to 1.24%. Yet a number of member states, the UK included, have rejected this idea before it's even been discussed.

\*\*\*

The European Parliament has decided to send a small delegation of MEPs to Guantanamo bay. The USA has finally agreed to it, albeit reluctantly. We have succeeded in keeping this issue on the agenda and making it clear that we regard it as an impediment to good transatlantic relations. My colleague Sarah Ludford has done excellent work on the issue. Yet it is very difficult to get US government people to focus on it. I hoped to raise it in my meeting this week with US Under Secretary of State for Humanitarian Affairs Paula Dobriansky, but she decided instead to give me a lecture about her country's plans for a global Community of Democracies. Since she arrived late and I had the Irish Justice Minister waiting, I did not push the issue with her. But I made sure the Irish minister knew the strength of my feelings, since he is the one dealing with the US on behalf of the EU.

\*\*\*

If proof were needed of the real nature of the United Kingdom Independence Party, it came this week when their SW Regional Organiser told a branch meeting on Monday that UKIP will not fight any by-elections before June in which the BNP is putting up a candidate. UKIP has recruited publicity guru Max Clifford to help in its campaign for the euro election in June. They will be throwing a lot of money at it.

\*\*\*

My weekend engagements include Woodspring constituency's Burns Supper, a debate at Bryanston School, a visit to the 90th birthday party of a Yeovil constituency stalwart and a photocall with David Laws. Last week I attended the Team for Cornwall meeting in Falmouth and Weston-super-Mare euro fundraiser. Next weekend I will be in Totnes for a photocall on Friday, then at a meeting with the Devon and Cornwall CBI; and on Saturday at the Devon and Cornwall Lib Dem regional conference followed by a Lib Dem Burns Supper in Frome.

I hope all my readers will be eating haggis too in memory of the great poet!

**Friday 30 January**

Our big event this week was the visit of UN General Secretary Kofi Annan to receive the European Parliament's Sakharov Prize on behalf of Sergio Vieira de Mello, the UN chief killed in the bomb attack on their Baghdad HQ last year. Annan is a man of great dignity and quiet persuasion. He said nothing in his acceptance speech of a role for the UN in Iraq, nor of its work in Cyprus or elsewhere. Instead he devoted the whole speech to the question of immigration. It was a powerful reproach to a European Union currently over-reacting hugely to the migration caused largely by the impact of western European trade sanctions on people's life chances in the developing world.

\*\*\*

Romania is also currently on our agenda. The European Lib Dem MEPs discussed on Wednesday whether to call for a suspension of accession negotiations since Romania is so far behind schedule in its bid to meet the criteria to join the EU. A large majority in the Group is in favour, though we have until Tuesday to make a final decision. Our Romanian Liberal sister party, the PNL, believes that only this kind of action will force their government to respect political pluralism and independence of the judiciary.

\*\*\*

Our Liberal colleagues in Gibraltar are rightly up in arms about the measure agreed in Parliament this week under the heading Single European Sky. This legislative package, steered through the House by my Dutch Liberal colleague Marieke Sanders, sees Member States merging their airspace sectors into new cross-border blocks. This should improve safety, cut delays and reduce emissions significantly. It also grants passengers rights to compensation in the event of over-booking by the airlines. However, Gibraltar has been excluded from the package. Spain refused to agree a deal which recognized Gibraltar, so the UK dropped its demand to include the Rock. Gibraltar could take the UK to the European Court of Justice for having denied its citizens, for reasons of political expediency, rights to which they are entitled.

\*\*\*

It pains me to return to the subject of MEPs pay and expenses. But reform-minded MEPs and most member state governments were left aghast this week when the German, French, Austrian and Swedish governments sabotaged an agreement which would have ended the practice of unjustifiably high expenses, in exchange for a common salary for all MEPs.

Why would they not agree to reform? Because MEPs opposed to reform planted stories in the popular press about how the new salary - 50% of the salary paid to a judge at the European Court of Justice - was an unjustifiable rise at a time of budget cuts at home. In fact, the new arrangement would have cost the taxpayer less. I am amazed that local MEP Caroline Jackson has the gall to say it was right to block the deal. Both she and I can in theory earn more from the current system than we would have earned from the new one. But the case for transparency of earnings is one I support, which is why all LibDem MEPs voted for it.

Where do we go from here? The ELDR Group will continue to lead the campaign for an end to the current expense arrangements. But the chances of a deal before the European election now look slim and once again the reputation of our institution will be dragged through the mud because British Tory MEPs and others rejected the chance to reform it.

**Saturday 07 February**

Preparations for ten new countries to join the EU on 01 May are almost complete. Nine of them have already nominated their candidate for the post of European Commissioner; these candidates will be grilled in a series of hearings in Parliament at the end of April. Pleasingly, there are two candidates from the Liberal family among them: Siim Kallas, a former Prime Minister of Estonia; and Janez Potocnik, who negotiated Slovenia's entry into the EU. I know Kallas well and have no doubt he will be a competent, if dry, official. This week I changed my flight home to allow me to stay in Brussels overnight on Thursday, where I had supper with Potocnik. Young, dynamic and enthusiastic, he'll be a star.

To my surprise, the European People's party (christian democrats and conservatives) used a conference in Brussels this week to launch a tirade against politicians from the new member countries who served as officials under communism. They discussed a proposal to ban from membership of the European Parliament anybody in this category. My view is that if somebody committed serious criminal offences under communism there may be a case to answer: but if we ban anybody who was in any way involved in the previous system of government we effectively exclude most qualified candidates over the age of forty, many of whom have done great service in steering their countries to democracy.

Moreover, the right wing have among their Observer MEPs almost as many people who served under communism as any other party. And they've some MEPs from western European countries who are using their current elected office to gain immunity from criminal charges at home. People who live in glass houses should beware of throwing stones.

More seriously, Romania is being hauled over the coals in Parliament for its failure to reform its former Communist ways. My colleague Emma Nicholson has tabled a motion in our Foreign Affairs committee calling for suspension of negotiations for Romania's membership of the EU. Emma's main concern is that the government has broken its promise to stop the sale of children for adoption. I have wider concerns too about corruption and lack of pluralism in political life and the state-controlled media. Whether or not the motion is adopted, her action has caused a great flurry of diplomatic activity in Romania. I hope it will lead to genuine reforms. In any case we must judge each candidate country on its merits. While any decision to suspend negotiations would require unanimity among EU member states, Parliament will have to vote its approval of Romanian membership in due course. The threat to turn them down may be our strongest weapon.

\*\*\*

The Rt Hon Paul Boateng MP, Chief Secretary to the Treasury, came to see me this week. He wants our support in amending the Investment Services Directive (on which the UK government suffered a rare defeat in the Council of Ministers) and in watering down the Temporary Workers Directive, which he claims will hit employment agencies. In fact he will have Lib Dem support on both, since my colleagues and I have discussed the proposals and reached the same conclusions as Whitehall. Ironically for the Minister, however, the Labour MEPs will take a different line from their government on temporary working. So the UK Labour government relies on the votes of LibDems and Tories in the EP to support their agenda.

\*\*\*

On Wednesday I led a conference on regional policy which we organised jointly with the European Free Alliance, a group of ten MEPs from Europe's stateless regions including the SNP and Plaid Cymru. The entry into force of the Amsterdam Treaty in 1999 gave the EU new powers in foreign policy and in justice and home affairs: one of the effects of this is that the regional policy agenda has slipped off the radar screen. Yet with ten new countries joining us, of which seven are smaller than Scotland, we need to address the question of how to deal with peoples who were casualties of the 300 year era of nation-state building.

Constituency engagements this weekend include meeting the Gloucestershire CBI, talks to schools in Wiltshire and Dorset, a meeting of the Lib Dem euro-election campaign team and a Lib Dem supper in Milborne Port. Next week Parliament is in Strasbourg and next Saturday (14 Feb) I look forward to delivering sweet words and romantic sentiments to the Yeovil Lib Dem supper.

**Friday 13 February**

Parliament had an unwelcome visitor this week in the form of President Uribe of Colombia. There was no need to invite the Colombian head of state to address us in what is called a 'solemn session': his predecessor Mr Pastrana came earlier during this Parliament. But the Socialist Group insisted and the European People's Party supported them (in exchange for socialist support for the invitation of the Croatian President).

Liberals, former Communists and Greens opposed the invitation, since Colombia has - in the words of the NGO Human Rights Watch - 'the worst human rights record in the western hemisphere'. The government responds to lawlessness with lawlessness: allows the army to assist paramilitary groups which murder, torture and rape with impunity; and has recently passed a law which allows people guilty of crimes against humanity to buy their freedom from prison.

We listened to what President Uribe had to say but declined to attend the lunch given in his honour. That afternoon we organised a meeting attended by over 200 people with speakers from human rights groups and others. The protests attracted more attention than the President's speech, so I think the visit backfired on him.

Other, more welcome, visitors were a group of students from Exeter University, to whom I spoke on Tuesday morning. They listened to me, to Glyn Ford MEP (Labour) and Caroline Jackson MEP (Conservative) and asked intelligent questions. When asked how many intended to vote in the European elections, however, fewer than a fifth of them put up their hands. And these are politics students!

\*\*\*

I am told that the main item on the news in the South West this week from the European Parliament was the Kindermann Report, a parliamentary initiative to reduce the slaughter of dolphins in fishing nets. I was interviewed at home on Sunday by Carlton Westcountry TV. It is an important subject: I've been putting down parliamentary questions for some three years now and last year the Commission actually got the matter on to the agenda at the Council of Fisheries Ministers (the regular meeting of the fifteen fisheries ministers in the EU's Council of Ministers). Little action was taken, however, so Parliament authorised Mr Kindermann to draw up proposals for action to put directly to the Ministers. The report contains a number of more-or-less sensible ideas, like extending the ban on drift nets of over two and a half kilometres in length to cover the Baltic Sea (they are already banned elsewhere), attaching 'pingers' to fishing nets to scare off dolphins and putting independent observers on board fishing boats at random to monitor their practices. But Parliament has no power to force the ministers to act: if they choose to ignore public opinion they are at liberty to do so, safe in the knowledge that national parliaments will hold them inadequately to account and that no TV camera will ever find its way into their meetings. Yet another example of why the European Parliament should have more powers?

\*\*\*

The most important item on our agenda this week was, I imagine, given very little media coverage in the UK. The Commission launched its proposals for the EU budget 2006-2011. The EU currently spends 1.07% of the Gross National Income of the Member States. The Commission says we need to increase this to 1.15% to pay for enlargement to ten or twelve new member states and to cover the new responsibilities which the EU has in foreign policy and in justice and home affairs. Seven chancellors of the exchequer (including Gordon Brown) have written a public letter demanding that the budget be capped at 1% of GNI, i.e. a cut in real terms. No matter that the same ministers decided less than two years ago to increase agricultural spending by 1% (meaning an increase to the EU budget of nearly 0.5%). Or that they make no proposals about where the cuts should fall; which doubtless they would be unable to agree. Popular Brussels-bashing, get-tough-on-spending politics prevails.

\*\*\*

On the Thursday afternoon of our Strasbourg session we debate 'urgency motions' on human rights. These are similar to early day debates at Westminster, having no legal force but nonetheless giving Parliament the chance to have its say. Often they make headlines in the country targeted and help to put pressure on human rights offenders. They provide a good opportunity for back-benchers to speak in the House and are not normally attended by party leaders.

I broke this convention yesterday when I tabled and took the floor on a motion condemning the Cambodian government for the extra-judicial killing of opposition leaders which is creating a climate of fear in negotiations between the parties on forming a government coalition. (Prime Minister Hun Sen lost the elections last year but is refusing to relinquish power to an all-party coalition government, which the opposition proposes.)

My determination to intervene stemmed from the murder a fortnight ago of Chea Vichea, a trade unionist in the garment industry and a founder member of the Sam Rainsy Party. I met him on my visit to Cambodia last April, when we addressed a rally together and chatted over lunch. He was a little younger than me, a charming man with a good sense of humour and a passionate commitment to democracy and good government. He was gunned down in broad daylight on 25 January in the street, in front of his wife and young daughter. So brazen were his attackers that passers-by mistook the bullet-shots for firecrackers. No condolences were forthcoming from the government and nobody has been arrested.

Parliament voted to call on the Commission to stop all non-humanitarian aid to the country until a legitimate government is formed.

Since I had to stay in Strasbourg on Thursday night I enjoyed the rare treat of finding time to go to the cinema. If you've not yet seen 'Bowling for Columbine', do.

**Monday 23 February**

The main item in - but not on - the EU's agenda this week was the three-nation summit which brought together France, Germany and the UK in Germany. At one time, Franco-German summits were the motor of developments in the EU: if France and Germany could agree, the others would all go along. Today they are more defensive in nature, designed to allow France and Germany to retain certain 'privileges' as large countries. The UK has been roped in since, in a Union of 25, more votes will be needed to form a 'blocking minority' to prevent certain developments. True, the three countries combined have nearly half the EU's population and probably two-thirds of its wealth. Agreement between them on the items on their published agenda - such as immigration, fighting crime and terrorism, economic growth - should be helpful. But other countries fear collusion of the 'Big 3' on the items on their unspoken agenda, such as who should be the next President of the European Commission and what secret deals can the three strike to protect important interests. Diplomacy, it may be. Diplomatic, it is not.

\*\*\*

Some quiet progress is being made on two urgent items on the EU's agenda. Talks on Cyprus have resumed with a view to reaching agreement to unite the island before 01 May, when - otherwise - only the Greek half will enter the EU. Or, more precisely under international law, Cyprus will enter the EU and a part of the EU's territory will be under Turkish armed occupation. The Turkish government is putting huge pressure on the Turkish Cypriots to reach agreement. Pressure on the Greek side is less obvious but, I am assured, is being applied. Time is short and the outcome uncertain. Success would bring huge relief in Brussels. As with the Northern Ireland peace process, EU money has already been earmarked for use to shore up peace through economic development.

The second item is the EU's draft Constitution. Since no agreement has been reached the intergovernmental conference is still formally in progress: the heads of state and government of the EU countries will meet again on 25 and 26 March to review progress made in talks between their officials. It is both possible and necessary to reach agreement before the June elections to the European Parliament. The few questions remaining to be resolved, such as the tussle over how many votes Spain and Poland should have in the Council of Ministers, are well known. The Irish Presidency has worked intelligently without opening this Pandora's box, and the EU could agree to delay the entry into force of any new distribution of votes in Council until 2009 or even 2014 if it helped countries to reach agreement. The EU's rules need revision to cope with a Union of 25 members. But the need in history does not always call forth its own fulfilment. If agreement is not reached by June we will have to soldier on with a system in logjam, unable to reach agreement on the kind of economic and other reforms which lay the basis for greater prosperity.

\*\*\*

My week started in Bristol, where Euro Prospective Parliamentary Candidate Kay Barnard and I met journalists to present our plans for June's election and to solicit their ideas about the likely level of press interest. To stress our intention to make this campaign an integral part of the Party's campaigning we took a leading PPC and a Bristol City councillor with us. We plan to arrange similar meetings in Plymouth, Gloucester and Bournemouth, but on the basis of Monday's I fear that journalists perceive little likely public interest in the campaign, other than how well the United Kingdom Independence Party might fare.

\*\*\*

I finished the week in Rome at a meeting on Friday with Christian Democrat MEPs who are thinking of leaving the European People's Party to join us. I did what I could to assure them of a warm welcome, to add fuel to their fears of greater eurosceptic tendencies in their party after June's elections and to convince them that they would be joining not the Liberal Group but a new formation of a different character. All of which is more or less true. But I must say that having served David Steel during the Liberal - SDP alliance days I had a strong sense of déjà vu! I may succeed in pushing up our numbers from the 55-65 I expect to 85 or even 95. But my optimism of the will is combined with at least some pessimism of the intellect.

## Friday 27 February

My week started on Sunday afternoon, when I flew to Bulgaria's sunny but snow-covered capital Sofia for meetings on Monday and Tuesday. Bulgaria's ruling coalition is formed by two Liberal parties: the National Movement Simeon II, led by the former monarch Simeon Saxe-Coburg-Gotha and the Movement for Rights and Freedoms led by Ahmed

Dogan. I met them both on Monday morning, followed by meetings with other leading representatives of both parties. They have had a roller coaster ride in government, having taken over a failing country just two and a half years ago with - in Simeon's case - a totally new party with virtually no experience of government and no real party structure. The MRF has provided a solid backbone of direction to the coalition while demanding little in return. They've succeeded in achieving 4% economic growth two years in a row, bringing down unemployment and reducing their public deficit to 6%, which is a major achievement. And though there are still problems of corruption and poor public administration to be overcome they are well on track to join the EU in 2007. I called for a formal de-coupling of Bulgaria and Romania, hitherto scheduled to join the EU together. The former will in all likelihood be ready; the latter probably not.

\*\*\*

Among many visitors to Brussels this week it was good to see Totnes PPC Mike Treleaven and his wife Elaine and constituency Chairman and spouse John and Sheila Stevens. It was John and Sheila's first visit, as part of a group organised by the admirable Lawrence Fullick on behalf of the Liberal Democrat European Group. Lawrence organises such visits regularly.

\*\*\*

On Wednesday I lambasted hapless Irish European Affairs Minister Dick Roche, who delivered on behalf of the Irish Presidency a statement about plans for the Spring economic summit next month. I told him that the EU's fledgling economic recovery should not be used as an excuse for delaying long overdue economic reforms. The EU's economy is embarrassingly uncompetitive compared to that of the USA and our influence in the world is reduced as a result.

\*\*\*

On Thursday we voted on a report on EU-Russia relations which instructed the Council and Commission to sort them out. A leaked internal memo on Monday had shown what Parliament has long suspected, ie, that we get very little influence for the diplomatic efforts we put in. A more robust approach is needed. I also recorded a TV interview for BBC TV's Brussels Week, but I suspect it will be screened at times (on Saturday, Sunday and Monday) and on channels with very few viewers.

\*\*\*

Today I will visit North Dorset, Poole and Bournemouth to campaign with our PPCs, ending with a speaking engagement for Christchurch Liberal Democrats. On Saturday I address the party's North West regional conference in Liverpool and then a Welsh Lib Dem supper. On Monday it's Wansdyke and Northavon followed by a media briefing in Gloucester and a flight back to Brussels. Hey, ho!

**Friday 05 March**

The process of making legislation is rather like making sausages: it looks messy, but generally the end product tastes OK. As the current European Parliament mandate draws to a close the sausage making machine is going into overtime to clear the kitchen before the election. So this week my European Liberal Democrat colleagues and I had to decide which way we will vote on a number of draft directives on our agenda for Strasbourg next week.

The one colleagues are being most heavily lobbied about is a draft Directive on intellectual property. The first draft of the bill would have made serious cross-border infringements of copyright and counterfeiting criminal offences, but national governments insisted that the EU has no competences to introduce such measures. The current proposal puts the onus on member states to take effective action against such infringements. The generic medicines lobby and some computer software people are unhappy with it, and they are people Liberals are sympathetic to. But I think their fears - about how the courts might interpret this legislation - are exaggerated. Companies trading in the EU's single market need cross-border protection for intellectual property and it seems to me that the new proposals, though not perfect, are workable and far preferable to not having legislation. This is a matter, however, where the Liberal Group cannot hope to amend the legislation, since a consensus has emerged between the moderate left and the moderate right which will in any case carry the day. We decided to join it.

\*\*\*

To what extent should food be able to claim health benefits in its labelling and advertising? In my constituency, some products of Wrigley's gum (in Plymouth) and the sugar free version of Ribena (Glaxo Smith Kline in Coleford in the Forest of Dean) are 'recommended' by the British Dental Association or other dental organisations; no doubt in return for a financial consideration. A draft European Directive seeks to limit the use of such endorsements and other claims about the nutritional or health benefits of food unless there is a proven case for making them. Readers' views would be appreciated.

\*\*\*

Two initiatives I took this week have enjoyed considerable press coverage in continental Europe but (to my knowledge) none in the UK. A public hearing which I hosted on Tuesday on the case for (or rather, the case against) biometric identifiers in passports attracted more attention than I expected. The USA currently offers visa free travel to the US to citizens of EU countries. They say they will withdraw this privilege with effect from 26 October unless EU countries put silicon chips containing biometric identifiers in their citizens' passports. These identifiers could be fingerprints or iris photographs or similar and are to be machine readable to help detect passport forgery and assist in the fight against terrorism. The spokesman from the US embassy who explained the proposal described it as no greater a change than when photographs were first used in passports, ie. a case of government taking advantage of new technology. Even if civil liberties concerns were satisfied, however - and if the US introduced strict enough data protection rules they might be, in my view - the potential for disruption of lives is huge. The technology required is expensive and relatively untested. And an error rate of just 0.5% would mean the detention, or barring from travel, of 5,000 passengers a week at Heathrow airport. I suspect my colleagues and I will be telling the European Commission to call the Americans' bluff on this one.

Which leads me to my second initiative. On Wednesday I chaired a conference on transatlantic relations with speakers including Romano Prodi, Francois Bayrou (French UDF party leader) and Solomon Passy (Bulgaria's foreign minister). One of the aims of this was to provide a platform for Prodi, Bayrou and me to appeal to moderate christian democrats (such as those in the parties led by Prodi and Bayrou) to leave the right wing European People's Party and launch a new centrist group in the European Parliament together with us. One reader has asked whether Christian Democrats are the sort of people who would be described as 'liberal', and expressed the view that surely there would have to be some common interest and shared values. Well, I am now at liberty to report that at a private meeting with Prodi and Bayrou in the margins of the conference I told them that Liberals would be interested in such an idea only on the basis of an agreed programme of priorities for the next parliament which would imply fairly substantial agreement on policy. I gave them each a draft 'ten point plan' on which I thought we might reach agreement. We've agreed to meet again before Parliament rises for the elections to discuss the matter further.

\*\*\*

Those who read Private Eye may have seen a piece (of which the details are substantially inaccurate but the essence is true) reporting that I am threatening Neil Parish MEP (Conservative, South West) with a libel action. He alleges - on his website and in an email newsletter - that I voted to include the EU 12 stars on the Red Ensign, which is an utterly scurrilous claim since in fact I voted specifically against the amendment which proposed this. I am not generally in favour of libel actions in politics, but his failure to desist from the claims is stoking my enthusiasm.

\*\*\*

On Friday I will be in Plymouth with PPCs Judy Evans and Karen Gillard, then in Bridgwater with PPC James Main and sea bass fishermen, in Weston-super-Mare to interview applicants for regional staff posts and then in Bridgwater again for a social event in the evening. On Saturday: Bridport, Taunton (euro campaign meeting) and Truro Lib Dems' annual dinner. On Sunday afternoon I travel to Stockholm where I address the Swedish Centre Party conference on Monday morning.

**Friday 12 March**

The European Parliament already has an end-of-term feeling about it. Though there are two more regular sessions of the full House (our Strasbourg weeks) to go - and a formal session at the beginning of May to welcome the new member states and approve their European Commissioners - our main debate this week was marked by the kind of party-political knock-about which is common at Westminster but rare to us. I used it to attack the Left's lack of leadership (they've just lost an election in Greece and are about to lose another in Spain) and the Right's current disunity over the development of the EU. I also challenged the Irish Presidency to raise the issue of Guantanamo at the forthcoming EU-US summit.

The Right's disunity also provided the subject of a lengthy discussion in the Liberal Group this week, when I sought - and obtained - a mandate from my colleagues to pursue talks with unhappy christian democrats and others about the possible formation of a new, stronger Centre Group in the next Parliament. Our Group was remarkably united, determined to form the bulk of any new Group and to insist on a credible policy platform, not just a vague commitment to greater EU integration.

\*\*\*

In preparation for the elections our Party's Federal Policy Committee met in London on Monday and signed off the final draft of the LibDem manifesto for the European elections. In my view it is the best manifesto we've ever fought on - and I've read them all since the first elections to the EP in 1979! It is constructive about the EU but also committed to improving it, inspiring but nonetheless realistic. Richard Grayson, the party's director of policy, has done an excellent job.

It surprises me therefore that there is so much pressure from the party in my South West constituency to fight this election on local issues. Make the EU relevant to local concerns, by all means; but don't pretend that a vote for the Liberal Democrats on 10 June will save a local hospital!

\*\*\*

My colleague Emma Nicholson MEP scored a great success this week when her report on Romania's progress towards joining the EU was approved by Parliament. The report sends a very clear message to Romania's socialist government that unless things improve fast we will not vote to approve their accession in January 2007.

\*\*\*

The ten terrorist bombs in Madrid on Thursday morning served as an awful reminder of how vulnerable society is to such outrages. When Parliament convened at 0900 our (Liberal) President Pat Cox made a statement condemning the attacks and expressing sympathy and solidarity with Spain. We observed a minute's silence. As the day went on, the toll of recorded deaths and casualties rose inexorably.

As I write this, we do not yet know who the perpetrators of the attack are. It seems likely to me that it was not planned solely in Spain. The European Parliament adopted a report two and a half years ago calling for more effective co-operation between the police forces, judicial authorities and intelligence services of the EU's member states to fight this kind of crime. I remember it well; I was the author of the report. My recommendations should be looked at again, for they are not yet all in place. Why? Because of something called 'national sovereignty'.

### Friday 19 March

Much attention has been paid this week to the lessons of the Madrid train bombs.

The first lesson is that the EU has failed to get its act together in fighting terrorism. The European Arrest Warrant proposal, a core plank of the anti-terrorism strategy, has been implemented by only 6 out of 15 member states despite an undertaking to have it in place by 01 January 2004. The 2001 EU action plan against terrorism, under which governments committed themselves to set up a unit of national anti-terrorist experts at Europol, has not yet been put into place. I know because I was the European Parliament's rapporteur on terrorism in 2001 and it was my job to secure parliamentary approval for these measures, which I did. The problem? The large member states will not trust each other enough to share criminal intelligence.

Last year the European parliament's rapporteur for the 2004 EU budget was a Dutch Lib Dem, Jan Mulder MEP. He and I worked to provide €9 million in the budget for co-operation between the criminal intelligence services of EU member states. The member states voted to reduce it to €1 million, so unconvinced are they of the need for such co-operation.

Reactions to the attacks have - predictably and depressingly - led to calls for new agencies and new supremos. We do not need them. We have agencies and functionaries galore. We just need the political will to allow them to work. How many more terrorist attacks will it take?

The second lesson is that the Spanish ruling party the Partido Popular snatched defeat from the jaws of victory by insisting that ETA was behind the attacks, when much of the evidence pointed to muslim extremists. If the voters believed it to be ETA, it would have helped the PP's re-election chances; if muslims it would re-ignite public outrage about Spain's participation in the invasion of Iraq. The government protested too much that it was ETA and were punished by the voters, the Socialists winning a clear victory.

\*\*\*

On Tuesday I received a petition with no fewer than 70,000 signatures gathered and presented to me by the UK Women's Institute. They were in support of the Commission's proposals for the registration, evaluation and authorisation of the tens of thousands of chemicals in daily use which have never been properly tested. Sperm counts in men and fertility rates in women are falling, quite probably linked to chemicals in our environment. Unless we are careful, we could inhibit within a couple of generations the ability of our species to reproduce. The chemical industry's lobby to gut the proposals is very strong. Thank heavens for the WI!

\*\*\*

The transport of animals was on the agenda in the agriculture committee this week. The committee voted to allow member states to take stricter steps to protect horses and ponies; and for a nine hour maximum journey time for animals destined for slaughter. Vehicles are to be certified and transporters to undergo training. When it comes to the floor of the House my colleagues will propose an amendment to limit the maximum journey time to eight hours. Let nobody say Parliaments are not responsive to public opinion.

\*\*\*

Consumer credit, greenhouse gases and lorry drivers' working hours were all subjects of draft legislation voted in committee this week. We will vote on them in plenary session in Strasbourg later this month or in April. This should be the final clearing of the decks before the June elections.

\*\*\*

I will be at Party conference in Southport this weekend. My speech to the conference rally will be available on my website. On Monday of next week I address a South West conference on EU funding in Exeter. On Tuesday I will present prizes at Chilton Cantelo school in Yeovil before travelling to Brussels. On Friday I will be in Ivybridge (speaking at a school), Clyst St Mary (addressing the Devon federation of WIs) and in Marlborough and Malmesbury for LibDem functions.

## Thursday 25 March

As I write this, as normal, on the flight back to Bristol on Thursday evening I guess I can predict what the UK media coverage of this week's European Council will be about. 'EU Governments take action on terrorism'. In reality there will be too little action. They committed themselves two years ago to implementing the European Arrest Warrant proposal (making extradition of suspected terrorists easier) by January 2004; thus far only eight out of fifteen countries have done so. They drew up an EU action plan against terrorism, no single component of which has been fully implemented yet. They agreed to get their anti-terrorist experts working together but are still jealously guarding the criminal intelligence each gathers. All of these might have prevented the attack on Madrid. If we are serious about fighting terrorism the time has come to set up a common criminal intelligence system. Now that would be a real breakthrough.

However they will make one good move in appointing Dutchman Gijs de Vries as their co-ordinator against terrorism to work alongside Javier Solana, the High Representative on Foreign and Security Policy. I've known Gijs since he was chairman of the Liberal Youth Movement of the EC back in 1980. When I was first elected to the EP he was our Group leader. Party members in Somerset may remember that he spoke at a euro-dinner in Glastonbury on 23 March 1996. He has a first class brain and an admirable capacity for work and is an inspired choice. And, as a true Liberal, he will be sensitive to civil liberties concerns.

\*\*\*

He will need to be. The pressure on us from the USA to give them 34 categories of information on each airline passenger flying into the USA, without data protection safeguards for the passengers concerned, is becoming intense. My Dutch Liberal colleague Johanna Boogerd MEP will recommend to parliament next week that we reject the deal proposed by the European Commission after negotiations with the Americans, reserving the right to refer it (under a new power gained by the European Parliament in the Nice Treaty) to the European Court of

Justice to assess how compatible it is with our data protection legislation. The lobbying from the US (and EU airlines, who want a quiet life) against her proposal is formidable. We got Johanna's recommendations through committee by 25 votes to 9 with 3 abstentions. I hope we can resist the pressure to defeat it on the floor of the House.

Why does the European Commission want a deal? Because the airlines have been supplying this information to the US authorities for some months now; without it, the US would not give them landing rights: they are almost certainly in breach of data protection laws and the European Commission should take them to court. They argue that we need a legal framework which will allow our airlines to fly passengers into the USA. What are our objections? 15 of the 34 categories of information requested by the US authorities are about behavioural characteristics of travellers (ie credit card statements). There is no mechanism for travellers to inspect and correct information, nor any redress if they are denied boarding of their flight. The number and type of US agencies who could gain access to the data is worrying and there is no limit to the length of time it can be retained. Moreover, only US citizens are protected by US data protection legislation. While we need to co-operate across the Atlantic in the fight against terrorism, this is going too far.

\*\*\*

The summit may well make progress towards the new EU Constitution. The Irish Presidency has been beavering away and it looks as if they now have sufficient agreement to re-open the inter-governmental conference (IGC) which failed in December, with a view to reaching agreement by the end of June. This will do more to help fight terrorism than anything which will be agreed this weekend, since it will give us (once it enters into force, i.e by June 2006 if we're lucky) the chance to take decisions on co-operation by qualified majority (ending the national veto) provided each new proposal also gains an absolute majority of votes (half the number of members, plus one) in the European Parliament.

\*\*\*

I spent Monday evening in London at the Party's Federal Executive Committee meeting, trying to make sure we fight a European election campaign which is honest about our policies. On Tuesday (my birthday) I spoke at Chilton Cantelo School's European Day. On Wednesday I addressed LibDem spokespersons from national parliaments, gathered in Brussels, on employment and social affairs; addressed business people at a lunch organized by online newswire EUpolitix; opened an ELDR hearing on the rights of the Roma people (there will be eight million in the EU after 01 May, equivalent to the population of Sweden or Austria; they are stateless and everywhere discriminated against); and acted as Quizmaster at a 'Liberal Democrat Brain of Europe' quiz. On Thursday I organized the meeting of six Lib Dem Prime Ministers and the Presidents of the European Commission and Parliament in advance of the EU summit. Friday starts in Langport and sees me in Ivybridge, Clyst St Mary, Marlborough and Malmesbury. On Saturday I travel to Killarney (and back!) to address the conference of Ireland's Progressive Democrats, a member party of the ELDR.

**Friday 02 April**

Our speaker, Pat Cox, presented a report on Wednesday on anti-semitism in the EU which makes harrowing reading. Together with Beate Winckler, head of the EU's monitoring centre on racism and xenophobia (a body I helped establish in my first parliamentary term), he launched the results of a comprehensive survey that shows anti-semitic tendencies - from minor verbal abuse to grievous bodily harm - to be high and rising in the four largest EU countries: Britain, France, Germany, and Italy. A minor row erupted when the Monitoring Centre decided not to publish an earlier report because they were unhappy about its methodology: this time there is no doubt that it is a serious and growing problem. (The report can be found at www.eumc.eu.int).

\*\*\*

Parliament also received a report this week from a committee set up to look into allegations by the Israeli Defence Forces that EU development aid funds are being channelled into terrorism by the Palestinian authority. In fact the report found no evidence that grant aid has gone anywhere but into the official accounts of the Palestinian authority; and no conclusive evidence that it was used to finance terrorism, though certain recommendations for better controls are made. The World Bank and the IMF were both involved in the investigation and were satisfied that the EU's policy was sound. The issue arises because in September 2000 the Israeli government froze the monthly transfer of tax revenues which they agreed to pay to the Palestinian Authority under the Paris Protocol. These accounted for two-thirds of the Authority's revenue and the EU decided to offer direct financial support to prevent the collapse of the Palestinian Authority. Clearly Israel did not like this. Its subsequent military iniatiatives have led to 39.4 million euros worth of damage to EU funded projects in Palestine.

\*\*\*

I've reported in previous newsletters about pressure from the U.S. authorities leading airlines to break European data protection laws by supplying them with all kinds of information about airline passengers. A report by my Dutch Liberal colleague Johanna Boogard MEP was approved this week and is a slap on the wrist for the Commission. But EU interior Ministers have decided that such information on travellers entering the EU from abroad would also help us in the fight against terrorism (though the type and amount of information they seek is far more modest). I therefore moved yesterday to ask the European Parliament to demand of the Commission that they negotiate a proper international agreement with the USA about the sharing of such data. This would need both EP and US Congressional approval, which would ensure that rules are in place to prevent an invasion of individual privacy unless there are clear grounds for suspicion of criminal activity of a serious nature: and even then, safeguards would be required. Thus far, the US administration has acted without explicit authorisation from Congress.

\*\*\*

MEPs are again in the headlines this week, especially in Austria and Germany, with "snouts in the trough" type allegations. An Austrian

MEP who was previously an investigative journalist decided to accuse his colleagues of signing in for their daily attendance allowances and then leaving - the 'sign in and sod off' principle. I've no doubt some do this, but from the MEPs I know I suspect it is a very small minority. Our rules could and should be changed to cut down any abuse of this type; but many Parliaments do not even require members to sign in!

\*\*\*

One piece of very good news. Commissioner Verheugen returned from the UN talks in Lucerne to tell us he is optimistic that the peace plan proposed for Cyprus will be accepted by both communities in the referendum on 24 April. The crucial difficulty has been property rights. Under the proposals non-Turks will be allowed to buy property in the Turkish Republic of Northern Cyprus when the average per capita income there has reached 85% of the level in the rest of the island; or after fifteen years, whichever comes first. There will be an international donors conference to raise money to help with the resettlement of displaced families and the EU's "acquis communautaire" (body of law) will be introduced gradually over two years from 01 May, when Cyprus joins us. The new United Cyprus Republic will have its own flag and national anthem. Of course, the Greeks may still vote against, which would be little short of tragic. But I think the plan gives enough to both communities to offer hope. I may well go there and campaign for a YES vote.

\*\*\*

One reader of these missives has suggested I collate them into a book for publication, which I will do over the summer. But I need suggestions for a title. My staff have come up with a number of ideas, ranging from the "EU've got mail" to "Waffles from Brussels". Any other ideas would be welcome.

\*\*\*

As it's Easter next week I shall be enjoying a couple of days break with my wife and children. Regular email service will resume on Friday 16 April.

## Friday 16 April

Parliament came back after the Easter weekend to a week of 'hearings' for the Commissioners-designate from the new member countries. A Commissioner proposed by a member state cannot take office until he or she has been approved by Council and Parliament. For Council this is normally a formality, since Council is composed of the governments who nominate these people. For parliament, they have to face a grilling by the members of the parliamentary committees to which they will report. In reality, we do not yet do this as intensely as the U.S. Congress. We have not yet declined to approve a nomination. But the day will come.

A fortnight ago a row broke out between Parliament and Commission on precisely this issue. Why? Because former Greek Commissioner Anna Diamantopoulou was recently elected to parliament in Greece and stepped down from her Brussels post. Her successor took the floor on behalf of the European Commission in a parliamentary debate before having been approved by parliament. MEPs naturally protested volubly.

Since then, French Commissioner Michel Barnier and Spanish Commissioner Pedro Solbes have accepted posts as government ministers in their home countries and have therefore resigned from the Commission, which now appears stricken with end-of-term exodus fever. Successors for both have been nominated and need to face parliamentary hearings in the three weeks we now have left before the House rises for the election.

My guess is we will vote to approve the ten new Commissioners who are due to take office on 01 May as ten new countries join the EU, and the successors for the departing Commissioners. In any case, these people will serve only until the end of the Commission's term in November. But I would not be surprised if our October hearings for the new Commission provided some upsets. And it would be no bad thing for European democracy.

\*\*\*

The pressure on MEPs to accept the Commission's recommendation to do a deal with the USA over data on airline passengers is becoming intense. It will come to a head in a vote on Tuesday on whether to refer the matter to the European Court of Justice. I am leading the fight to have the Commission withdraw its proposal and seek a proper international agreement with the US, with data privacy safeguards, thus obviating the need for us to go to law. I've made a number of phone calls to Commissioners today. Am I naive to think that I may yet win? It will be close.

\*\*\*

Cyprus is our biggest headache at present. The United Nations' Special Envoy to Cyprus, Alvaro de Soto, addressed our foreign affairs committee this week and said that the plan has been presented by the UN, as agreed, because the Leaders of the Greek and Turkish Cypriot communities were unable to reach agreement themselves. Indeed, he told us, there is little hope they would reach agreement even if they had an infinite amount of time available. The decision to put the plan to a referendum was agreed by the Cypriot parties with the strong backing of Greece and Turkey; all were consulted before the date was set. But both Mr Denktash and Mr Papadopoulos are urging their people to vote No. The referendum on 24 April on the Annan plan looks set to be approved by the Turks but rejected by the Greeks. Which will mean that Cyprus will enter the EU with a part of EU territory occupied by foreign troops. This is a disaster of our own making, yet nobody in the EU seems prepared to show the leadership needed to press the two communities to find a solution. Everyone wants it to be Kofi Annan's problem at the UN, not a European responsiblity. Some Greeks talk of postponing the referendum. I think we should be postponing Cyprus' entry to the EU.

\*\*\*

I spent Tuesday in Hungary, campaigning with our Liberal SDS friends there in Budapest and in Veszprem. The number three candidate on their list is an impressive woman from the Roma minority whose election would be a real boost. Of all the EU accession countries, Hungary has perhaps the fewest problems. They will make an excellent contribution to the EU from day one.

\*\*\*

On Friday I will be campaigning in Taunton and in Plymouth and on Saturday at LD social events in North Devon (West Yeo) and in Exeter. Plans for our Lib Dem European election campaign seem to be proceeding apace. I know the Tories are getting into gear too because they are writing letters to the regional and local papers attacking me. If readers see such letters and feel minded to reply in my support I would be deeply grateful.

**Saturday 24 April**

Thank you to those readers who offered suggestions for the title for a book to collate these newsletters. My favourite thus far is "EU've Got Mail", but I'm still mulling it over.

\*\*\*

This week was our last legislative session in Strasbourg before the European election. We managed to debate and vote on a massive 85 reports, compared to 40-45 in a normal week. One was a draft directive (first reading) on the safe disposal of batteries, which are currently rarely collected and recycled but either dumped with other rubbish (putting highly toxic substances into soil and groundwater), or incinerated, releasing toxins and heavy metals into the air. If collected and recycled, iron, nickel and silver can be recovered. Though battery collection boxes are a familiar sight in Belgium, only industrial and vehicle batteries are recycled in the UK. We voted for a minimum of 50% of all household batteries to be collected for recycling within 5 years. We also called for the long term replacement of all nickel-cadmium and lead batteries by less toxic alternatives. Cadmium is a carcinogen that accumulates in the human body.

\*\*\*

Three initiatives which Liberal Democrats took in Parliament came to fruition this week. 1) Recommendations on improving safety at sea, drawn up by our committee of enquiry on the sinking of the 'Prestige' - the enquiry the Spanish right-wing tried to block - were approved by Parliament. 2) In a heated vote in which most Conservatives refused to take part, our recommendations on media pluralism were approved after the most blatant filibustering I have ever seen was attempted by Mr Berlusconi's Forza Italia MEPs. Their wrecking tactics included the theft of documents from a committee room in which amendments were printed and then an attempt to use our standing orders to stop the vote on the grounds that amendments were not available in all the official languages. Of course the report was critical of Berlusconi, but it was also a balanced report drawing attention to Europe-wide aspects of concentration of ownership of media outlets. A shocking illustration of the problem came to our attention this week when the President of Cyprus ordered the TV not to give airtime to Yes campaigners in their referendum. 3) Parliament voted, by a margin of 16 votes, to refer to the European Court of Justice the Commission's proposed deal with the USA on transfer of data relating to airline passengers. This has been a personal crusade of mine and gives me great satisfaction.

\*\*\*

The biggest UK news of the week was of course Blair's decision to hold a referendum on the new EU Constitution. It is an astute (if risky) move in domestic political terms. I welcome it because I think we need the debate and the subsequent exorcism. But from a European perspective it has rendered more difficult the ratification of the new Constitution since it ups the pressure on other countries also to stage referenda. I'd like to see a EU-wide poll, held on the same day right across the continent. Then we'd have a truly "European" debate.

## Friday 30 April

It seems perhaps I was naive. At least to forget that it is never all over until the fat lady sings. In the ongoing saga regarding the passing of data on airline passengers to the US authorities, Europe's governments have found a way of forcing the issue back on to Parliament's agenda. The legal services of the Council, in which the member state governments are represented, have found a procedural mechanism by which they can force us to vote again on the issue next week. By then, Parliament will have 162 new members from the countries which join us on 01 May. They will be more susceptible to pressure from their governments, or so the Council believes. So a parliament session next week which was supposed to be purely ceremonial will be turned into another show of force between EU governments and MEPs over the balance between civil liberties and the fight against terrorism.

\*\*\*

On Wednesday I was in London and used the opportunity to attend a reception given by the P.M. to celebrate enlargement of the EU. It coincided with a visit to London by our speaker, Pat Cox. I tried to get across to Blair and his people the need to fight two campaigns to win the referendum on the new EU Constitution. The first should be the European Movement/Britain in Europe campaign to set out the factual case. But we also need what I dubbed the 'provisional wing' of the YES campaign: a group of experienced campaigners who know all the tricks and who can fight a campaign for the hearts of the British people. Because the NO campaign will do precisely that.

\*\*\*

On the plus side this week we had an excellent ELDR rally on Thursday in Brussels to launch our European election campaign. Three of our prime ministers were in attendance and all spoke well, as did Charles Kennedy. Nearly 500 people attended, most of them candidates for election in June. I urged people to remember to keep ideals and passion in their campaigns. (My speech can be found at www.eurolib.org.)

It looks as if we will do well on 10 June. Not just in the UK, but across the continent. I met again this week the leaders of other parties who may join us after the election to form a larger centre force in the European Parliament and we are making good progress in our ambitions.

\*\*\*

Paul Tyler MP and Colin Breed MP joined me in Brussels on Tuesday to meet Commission officials about Objective One funding for Cornwall. I am optimistic we will secure its continuation, though if Gordon Brown gets his way there will be no more structural fund spending in western Europe. On Friday I go with Paul to visit the Davidstow creamery, an excellent example of how this funding can be used to support the local economy. I'll then travel on to a meeting with all our Cornish MPs and later address a Lib Dem supper in Truro constituency.

On Saturday I visit a cider maker in North Somerset to discuss the threat to orchards from the government's implementation of the CAP reform (only in England has the government chosen to disadvantage orchard owners); to Bristol for a Euro-election 'Get-the-vote-out' launch and then to our Campaign Team meeting for the euro election.

**Saturday 08 May**

Parliament rose on Wednesday after only three days in Strasbourg - an unusually short week. The sitting was essentially a formal one. We had to verify the credentials of 162 new MEPs who now represent the ten new member countries and approve the nomination of ten new Commissioners. I put them on notice that the Liberal Group feels our approval hearings are not rigourous enough and that when we hold hearings in October for the twenty five Commissioners who will make up the next Commission they can expect tough questioning from us.

\*\*\*

One item of business of a normal legislative nature which was forced onto our agenda this week by the member state governments was their request for urgent consideration of the proposed deal on passing information about transatlantic airline passengers to the US government (see previous recent newsletters). The governments believed that a new parliamentary majority (i.e. a parliament with 162 new members) would agree to a measure which we had decided ten days earlier to delay by referring it to the European Court of Justice for their opinion. I feared we could lose the whole thing and was immensely proud when on Tuesday Parliament followed my advice (by 343 votes to 301) to refuse to put it on the agenda. (The personal letter from me to each of the 162 new members on Monday may have helped.) I believe our governments intend to go ahead and do the deal with the USA in any case, but the Court of Justice will consider the matter on 06 June and could well declare their action illegal.

\*\*\*

A report from Parliament's secretariat this week makes interesting reading. In some areas of EU legislation, Parliament enjoys co-decision with the member states represented in the Council. In other words, they cannot act unless we agree. This week's report shows that over the five year term of this Parliament an average of 81 legislative acts every year were passed under co-decision. That's two a week when Parliament is in session. Two-thirds of all these laws were successfully amended by MEPs.

What are all these laws? Take, for example, the Blood Products Directive. This standardises the quality rules for blood collected by transfusion services in each member state, so that if a British tourist in Spain has an accident s/he can be sure that the quality of blood they receive will be the same as in the UK, and if there is a terrorist attack on a city in Britain extra blood supplies can be flown in from capitals across the EU. That's an example of the EU adding value.

\*\*\*

Over the past two weeks I have taken part - with the leaders of the other parties in Parliament - in televised debates about the European elections for national television in Sweden, Finland, Greece and Germany. On TV in other member sates there is regular reporting about EU affairs. Yet a recent report in the UK found that only a tiny percentage of the BBC's political coverage is about the EU. Will this change? Perhaps a little. I think the BBC was rather stung by this report. So BBC breakfast TV will show a series of small pieces next week about the EU. With any luck, it may catch on.

\*\*\*

The political highlight of my week was welcoming (to my regular Wednesday lunchtime meeting with Commissioners from the Liberal family) the three new Liberal Commissioners: Siim Kallas of Estonia, Janez Potocnik from Slovenia and Marcos Kyprianou from Cyprus. Pavel Telicka from the Czech Republic also joined us, at his request. For the past five years we've had only Bolkestein and (occasionally) Prodi. We're a political family with growing influence.

The personal highlight was taking delivery of a new car in Belgium, which I have bought for 25% less than it would have cost me here. In the two days each week which I spend travelling around my constituency I manage to clock up over 22,000 miles a year. Which perhaps suggests I hardly deserve the plaudit that Friends of the Earth have given me as the region's 'greenest' MEP (see www.foe.co.uk). But in a vast and largely rural constituency stretching from the edges of the New Forest up to Stow on the Wold and down to Scilly, I've sadly few transport options.

\*\*\*

In the constituency I addressed meetings last weekend in Truro and Weston-super-Mare and visited the new Dairy Crest creamery at Davidstow in Cornwall. This week I've presented Corporate Social Responsibility awards to employees of Barclays bank, visited Somerset's stunning Ham Wall nature reserve (top marks to the RSPB), spent four hours delivering leaflets in Plymouth, spoken to Taunton constituency Lib Dems and addressed a Somerset CC twinning conference.

Next week I'll be on the continent and then from 17 May to 10 June here, campaigning in the European election campaign. There'll be no more weekly newsletters until after the election, I'm afraid; but if you're really keen, my campaign press officer is trying to convince me to write a daily web-log of the campaign and I'll let readers know where it can be found.

# Appendix

### I. Speeches to Parliament on the Stability & Growth Pact (i), and on enlargement (ii).
*Letter of 25 October 2002*

**(i)** Commission President Mr Prodi described the Stability and Growth Pact last week as 'stupid, like all decisions which are rigid'. Commissioner Lamy is also on record as having described the pact as 'medieval'. Aside from the questionable wisdom of using such strong language, especially to a newspaper from the country which is doing the most damage to what remains of the credibility of the Stability Pact, one begins to wonder whether this is part of an orchestrated campaign.

My question to the Commission President is this: in making your remarks to Le Monde - and you have said that you stand by every word - was it your intention to launch a debate on how to reform the Stability and Growth Pact? If so, that is a debate we welcome, but surely a debate which would better have been conducted some months ago. Had the Commission acted more firmly then, using the licence that we gave you when we invested you, its own authority and that of the Stability Pact might have suffered less damage.

In the current circumstances, no change is clearly not an option, but two principles must guide us. The first is that a well-run economy and a stable currency require taxes and spending to be in balance over the course of the business cycle. The second is that the rules are the same for all countries, large or small. Those principles are at the heart of the Stability Pact and my group expects them to be the starting point for any reform.

If today marks the beginning of a debate on how to improve and strengthen the Pact, what reforms do we need to give it renewed credibility? First of all let us be clear on what we should not do. We should not call into question the 3% limit for deficits as we hit hard economic times. If countries do not pay off their debts, then we will all pay the price in higher interest rates and a weaker currency.

The Liberal Group agrees with Mr Prodi that the Stability Pact must be applied intelligently. That is why we supported the Commission's decision to allow two more years for countries to return their budgets to balance, because growth had been slower than expected. But we must not forget that postponement to 2006 came with strings attached in the form of a requirement to reduce structural deficits by 0.5% year on year. The Liberal Group believes that a new target for the structural deficit should be included in the Stability Pact. That would increase pressure on governments to reduce their deficits in their good times so that they can allow borrowing to take the strain when times are bad.

On that analysis, any intelligent interpretation would clearly conclude that France's recent budget makes no effort to reduce its structural deficit and is clearly in breach of the Stability Pact. France must therefore face an early warning. That is what we would like to hear from the Commission today. When the Commission brings forward a proposal for such an early warning, then it will help to restore credibility to the Pact.

The Liberal Group agrees with you, Mr Prodi, that the Stability and Growth Pact needs authority behind it to apply it. That is why we call for the Commission to have the power to issue early warnings against countries which are breaching the rules, whether finance ministers agree or not. Only if the Pact has a strong policeman can Member States be forced into taking corrective action while they can afford to.

Let us be clear. We will not support any reforms to the Stability and Growth Pact which undermine the basic principles of fiscal responsibility and equality before the law. The end point of reform must be a strengthened Stability Pact which punishes fiscal largesse and rewards countries which run their budgets responsibly. Judging by the warm welcome which Francis Mer, the French finance minister, gave to your remarks in that interview, I fear that France will feel empowered to flout the rules. If you wish to have the authority to enforce the Stability Pact, then you must earn that authority by acting promptly against France and any other countries which might be tempted to follow their example.

\*\*\*

**(ii)** Mr President, if the Treaty had been rejected by your countrymen, this week's Council would have been marred by recrimination and disarray. Due in no small part to your efforts, Ireland's 'yes' vote has put us back on track for Europe to be reunited in 2004.[1]

The decisions that remain will not be easy. As our esteemed former colleague the President-in-Office[2] has said, decisions involving money rarely are. But the Heads of State and Government must not allow themselves to flunk this historic opportunity by fighting over how to pay the bill.

My group believes that enlargement can be financed under the financial arrangements agreed in Berlin. Some shifting between the different headings should be possible, within the overall limits. The final package must guarantee that new Member States will not be net contributors before 2007. Otherwise we will feed resentment and face the risk of more cliff-hanger referenda in the aspirant countries.

Inevitably, the major area of disagreement is the common agricultural policy. While the Liberal Group does not regard CAP reform as a precondition for enlargement, it is clear that significant reform of our farm policies is essential to the success of enlargement and also for other reasons.

I hear that President Chirac expects the United Kingdom to bring its budget rebate into play, while he refuses to countenance reform of his farm policies before 2006. We support the Commission's proposals to phase in income support to farmers for the new Member States, but we also expect all existing Member States to commit themselves to far-reaching reform of the CAP, as proposed in the mid-term review.

The second major area of concern is the readiness of the applicant states to live within the disciplines of the single market and respect the European Union's values. We share the concern expressed in the Commission's progress report about corruption in a number of these countries and the need for progress in implementing EU legislation, particularly in the field of justice and home affairs. That is why it is right that there should be a reinforced monitoring system to ensure that countries fulfil their commitments.

The President of the Commission called for enthusiasm and intelligence. Commissioner Verheugen's approach has demonstrated the latter, but a touch more enthusiasm in the Council for enlargement and for the new Europe it heralds would not go amiss.

[1] *Graham was addressing Irish Liberal President Pat Cox. Ireland had just voted in a second referendum on the Nice Treaty, which aimed to reform the institutions to allow for enlargement of the Union from 15 to 25. The 'YES to Nice' vote received 62.89% of the vote.*

[2] *Bertel Haarder, the Danish European Affairs minister, was a Liberal MEP from 1994-2001.*

*EU've got mail!*

## II. Speech to Liberal Democrat Autumn conference, Brighton 2003
*Letter of 26 September 2003*

Fellow Liberal Democrats,

The debate we've just had about our platform for the European elections shows three things: that we've a first class team of Liberal Democrat MEPs from the UK and good new candidates in place; that we are the party of pro-European reform in this country; and that on rare occasions it is possible for we Brits to have a sensible debate on Europe!

From the venomous headlines in some of our newspapers you might think such debate impossible. Headlines like the Daily Mail's "We obey the rules while others cheat". Last Saturday the Today programme told us that Brussels is bullying Britain into VAT on children's clothes. Talk about sexing up their stories! If the factual flaws were not bad enough, persistently the press panders to prejudice. Liberal Democrats seek to root it out.

The history of the Liberal enlightenment is a succession of battles against prejudice - ethnic, religious, racial and other - and the European Union is a weapon in these battles.

It's a powerful weapon too. It brought together France and Germany after the war. From six countries at the start it grew to nine in the 1970s, to twelve in the 80s and fifteen in the 1990s. Next year we take in ten new members, closing the chapter on communism and the Cold War.

With each enlargement the new Europe grows stronger, and the weight of the big countries less decisive. We're all minorities now, even if some countries don't like to admit it. We have to think in terms of co-existence and co-operation, rather than might is right.

Europe will go on to take in Romania, Bulgaria and Turkey. The carrot of Union membership is so tempting that Turkey has seen rapid change from autocracy to democracy. And in due course the countries of the western Balkans will join us, and Switzerland, Norway and Iceland too.

*Appendix*

On Saturday, supposedly sceptical Latvia voted Yes. Why? Because for Latvia's 2 million people, the difference between the European Union to their West and their experience with the East is like the difference between a jacket and a strait-jacket!

Ten new countries set to join the EU next year, with more to come. The European ideal still has the capacity to inspire. Which is just as well, because we need the EU if we're to take on the big challenges confronting humankind.

Challenges such as a rapidly growing world population, where more and more leave their home countries to escape war or hunger or sheer hopelessness.

Challenges like coping with the consequences of climate change on air and water and soil.

Or tackling internationally organised crime, where some criminal gangs are more powerful than some national governments, funded by the trafficking of drugs and weapons and art treasures - to say nothing of the trafficking of people - and increasingly in touch with terrorists.

None of these are problems that one country can tackle alone. Indeed, none of them can be tackled except by democracies with good governance, market economies and respect for the rule of law.

This is what the EU offers. The vision of its founding fathers was maybe more modest. They wanted peace and secure food supplies. Their success has spurred our generation of Europeans to rise to the new challenges of globalisation.

We lock our economies together to provide prosperity. We strive for freedom of movement to open opportunities. Increasingly, we work side by side in search of security. That's why Blair was in Berlin[1].

Of course, it doesn't always work. Sweden said No to the euro. Why? Partly because recession is causing pain in the euro zone. But largely because the social democrats failed to convince their compatriots that a common currency is just part of a wider patchwork of peace and progress. The euro does what the gold standard, Bretton Woods and the EMS tried to do: it gives us a stable framework for trade. And trade generates wealth.

The Swedes should have heeded Lloyd George's dictum: 'The hardest way to cross a chasm is in two leaps.' Because if losing investment at home and influence abroad does not make them think again, the next torrent of turmoil on the money markets will.

It's the same for sterling. Which word do people associate most often with sterling? "Crisis"!

Europe was also at sixes and sevens over Iraq. But the embarrassment of disarray has hastened the day when we speak with one voice in foreign affairs.

Of course the EU will help Britain and America to extricate themselves. As least as bad as the butcher of Baghdad would be the Tikrit Taliban. But if we want to ease the pressure, where the tectonic plates of Christianity, Judaism and Islam grate perilously against each other, we need the world with us.

And this is the fundamental challenge. Our planet provides just one bed to harbour different dreams. If one rolls over, another falls out.

That's why George Bush is wrong to go it alone. Not just in Iraq, or even Kyoto. Wherever you look, the US is in isolation. From the International Criminal Court to the Ottawa Land Mines Convention, from the chemical weapons talks to the UN Convention on the rights of the child. (Do you know why they won't sign the children's convention? Because it disallows the death penalty for under eighteens. One state sentences at sixteen: George Bush's torrid Texas.)

In contrast, the European Union is so opposed to the death penalty that doing away with it is one of the pre-conditions for membership.

While Britain has hacked away at its Human Rights Act in the fight against terrorism, the EU anchors human rights at the centre of its new constitution. And we will persist in pressing our partners in America about the plight of the Palestinians and the prisoners in Guantanamo Bay. These wrongs wreak the rainfall of revenge which fills the tributaries of terror.

A new international approach must be based on respect and understanding, on the force of argument, not on the argument of force. We must not let the threats we see blind us to the apparent menace we pose. Peace can only prosper in a climate in which the hurts of nations can heal.

The EU has done just that for the aggressors and the victims of two European wars. Now we have to do it beyond our borders.

But reconciliation starts with justice. One billion of our fellow citizens worldwide live on less than a euro a day. Yet every cow in Europe gets a subsidy of two euros a day. Where's the justice in that?

Europe must reform a farm policy with obscene effects.

Compassion apart, Liberal Democrats see that unless we open our markets to developing countries' products, we will take their people.

Sadly, the world trade talks failed in Cancún. Trade is the most powerful potion against poverty. An agreement would have made trade fairer and we must try again. But we will continue to back the WTO because the trade talks of today are better than the trade wars of yesterday.

On the euro, on Iraq, on trade the EU's weaknesses are exposed. Yet they do not call into question the importance of European government.

Liberals understand this, which is why we are on the up across Europe. In the Union and its candidate states we have five Liberal Prime Ministers. Liberals are in government in 11 countries. We have a Liberal President of the Commission. And of the European Parliament, where my 53 MEPs hold the balance of power. Liberal Democrat votes are making the difference the length and breadth of Europe.

Nobody pretends the EU's perfect. Government at EU level is often no better than government at national or local level. But it is normally no worse either.

Just like at home, Liberal Democrats in Europe are at the forefront of reform. We want to bring government closer to the people. We want to cut red tape, open up government to public scrutiny, to fight fraud. That's why I insist that the EU's Economics Commissioner resigns if suspicions of fraud in his department are confirmed.

And because we believe in Europe, our criticisms carry more weight. This country's conservatives, constantly carping, are held in contempt. So reform of Europe needs more Liberal Democrat MEPs.

The new EU constitution shows how Liberals are respected. Our members of the drafting Convention insisted it contain a bill of rights. We succeeded. We secured a secession clause, paving a legal path for a country to withdraw from the EU if it chooses. We put more policy-making under the purview of Parliament. Its a credible Constitution and deserves debate. The British government refuses us a referendum. I suppose after last Thursday they'll want to refuse us by-elections[2].

But to escape from disappointment, Britain need not court disaster. Tories tell us this Treaty would betray our birthright. But if it is a blueprint for tyranny, why did the Conservative MP on the Convention sign up to it?

Its the oldest Tory trick. Protest in public, sign on the dotted line in private.

Why do they always sign up? Because, like the slogan on the free condoms I helped hand out in Estonia two weeks ago for their referendum: "it's better to be inside".

*Appendix*

It is better to be inside.

But not just for business.

It's better to be inside for the junior doctors and the shift workers deprived of decent rest times in the UK.

It's better to be inside for the children at risk of asthma craving clean air to breathe.

Its better to be inside if you're waiting for an operation in Bedford and there's a bed free in Bordeaux.

And it's better to be in the EU, fighting for British interests in Europe, than clamouring that the continentals should be more like us.

Remember that line sung by Flanders and Swann: 'The English are moral, the English are good, and clever, and honest - and misunderstood.'

Of course we love our stereotypes. And after 50 years of Europe the French are no less French, the Italians no less Italian and the British no less British. But together we make up more than the sum of our parts.

What's more, we're winning that old battle against prejudice. Not because the world's favourite rapper is white; our most famous golfer is black; the England manager is a Swede and Switzerland holds the America's Cup.

But because the European Union deals daily with prejudice. EU troops police ethnic conflict in Macedonia. We've abolished the upper age limit for applying for jobs in the Commission. EU rules protect the Roma and other minorities from persecution.

Turning the page of history from the blood-spattered chapter of the past needs a strong EU. Building a stable, just and peaceful future calls for common commitment now. Peace, prosperity, opportunity. At home,

*EU've got mail!*

those are Europe's achievements. Abroad, those must be our goals.

[1] *Prime Minister Tony Blair was in Berlin for trilateral talks with Chancellor Gerhard Schroeder and French President Jacques Chirac on 20 September 2003. It was the first meeting of the three largest players in the EU since the end of the Iraq war. Discussions centred around the role of the UN in post-war Iraq, and the length of time before sovreignty should be handed over to the Iraqis.*

[2] *Liberal Democrat Sarah Teather had just won a landslide victory at the Brent East by-election on 18 September. Traditionally a Labour stronghold (at the last election Labour won with 63.2% of the vote), Sarah won by a margin of 1,118, polling almost 40% of the votes.*

## III. Speech to ELDR Congress, Amsterdam 2003
*Letter of 17 November 2003*

Fellow Liberal Democrats
Fellow Europeans

Thank you for an excellent congress. To our hosts from VVD and D66, may I extend on behalf of all of us our warm thanks for their hospitality. To all of you, thank you for a lively, intelligent, good-natured debate.

This week's debate on our manifesto for next year's European elections confirms one thing for me.

That we are the European political alternative. In this party, you can have a sensible discussion about the kind of Europe we want. You can talk about the issues without prejudice or caricature. You stand and you fall on the power of your argument.

It's a character of this party that serves us very well in Brussels and Strasbourg.

Liberals hold the balance of power in the European Parliament, where our arguments command respect. Studies by the London school of Economics show that the ELDR wields influence in the European Parliament out of all proportion to its size.

As my predecessor Pat Cox used to put it: we punch above our weight.

It is the Liberals Democrats and Reformers who make the difference.

In this parliament we made the difference on public health. We voted to make Europe's cigarette manufacturers cut tar and nicotine levels and put clear health warnings on all their packaging.

In the face of fierce lobbying, we made the difference on consumer safety. Genetically modified food in Europe is now subject to the world's strictest labelling requirements. That means choice for customers.

We made the difference on the environment. We voted to force EU governments to honour new targets for renewable energy.

We made the difference on enlargement. When the time came to welcome the new member states, only European Liberals voted unanimously to do so.

We made the difference on economic reform. We demanded a more open and accountable Commission and European Central Bank. We voted to further open the European market in services. That means new investment, more competition and more choice.

We made the difference on the Convention on the Future of Europe. We demanded a Bill of Rights - the Charter of Fundamental Freedoms - at the heart of our new political contract. We got it.

We made the difference in democratic accountability. We helped produce a European Constitution that would dramatically increase the power over policy-making of elected representatives in the European Parliament.

In Pat Cox we gave that Parliament its first Liberal President in over twenty years. Pat has carried our Liberal message to the highest levels of the European Union.

These are our achievements. But what of our future.

For Liberals history is a succession of struggles against prejudice - religious, ethnic, racial, gender or other. For Liberals the European Union is a weapon in this struggle.

With each enlargement we get collectively stronger, even as the weight of our national divisions diminishes. In the new Europe we are all minorities, even if some of our larger nations haven't grasped this yet. From now on we can think only in terms of coexistence and co-operation. Proceed only in concert.

Next year's European elections have to be about Europe's added value. For far too long European elections have been simply another chance to deliver punches in domestic politics. Next year we all have a responsibility to raise the level of debate about Europe.

It is sometimes said that the EU has no "demos". No electorate. Brits are Brits, Greeks are Greeks and Finns are Finns.

But there is a European 'street'. How do we know? Because this year Europeans poured into it and spoke with one voice, over the heads of their squabbling governments, about the war in Iraq.

The Convention on the Future of Europe may not have caught the imagination of Europeans. But the Constitution it produced has. Eurobarometer figures released this week show that almost 70% Europeans believe Europe needs such a constitution. Four out of five want a say in this process through a referendum.

This public sense of Europeanness must be grasped and nurtured.

If Europeans want a say on the Constitution, there should be an advisory referendum, held on the same day as the European elections.

The German writer Gunther Grass once said that the job of a citizen is to keep his mouth open. We must encourage Europeans to think and talk and argue about Europe.

More than ever, we must all be activists now.

Why now more than ever?

Because the European Union is about to get bigger, and as it gets bigger the importance of connecting it to Europeans becomes more crucial than ever.

Why now more than ever?

Because globalisation and increasing interdependence are raising the stakes for all of us.

The world outside Europe is pushing against us insistently. Europe faces new threats and new challenges.

New challenges like a growing world population, where more and more leave their homes to escape from war or hunger or sheer hopelessness.

Or challenges like easing the tensions where the tectonic plates of Islam and Judaism and Christianity grind against each other.

New threats like internationally organised crime, where some criminal gangs are more powerful than some national governments.

Or threats like climate change, and our impact on our shared planet.

New realities, like the way money and information move faster than ever before.

These are challenges that no one country can tackle alone. They can only be confronted by countries with common values, working together.

So we lock our economies together to provide stability and prosperity.

We work side by side in search of security.

We insist on a fairer world, and a society that takes sustainability seriously.

We translate our combined weight into influence where it matters most: in the UN, the WTO, the corridors of the White House.

When the European Union fails we all fail.

Europe failed to live up to its own economic rules. France and Germany preached allegiance on the Growth and Stability Pact. And then practised contempt. Contempt for Europe's credibility. Contempt for those who play by the rules. Contempt for the need to make convergence work. Sweden's voters were decidedly unimpressed[1]. Who can blame them?

Europe failed in Cancun[2], where its indefensible Common Agricultural Policy continued to make a mockery of our grand words about helping the third world rise out of poverty. One billion people on this planet get by on one euro a day. Every European cow gets a subsidy of two. Where is the success in that kind of injustice?

Europe failed to find a common approach in Iraq. It stood sidelined and Britain and the United States and their coalition of the willing or the arm-twisted blundered into war and occupation. The cost of building democracy in Iraq will be high, as Italy tragically discovered this week[3]. The cost to Europe of failure would be infinitely higher.

Too often Europe's potential is squandered by vested interests and bad national habits. If Europe is to move on from these failures to a more successful future we have to learn from them.

Learn that if we don't stand together on foreign affairs, we will fall apart. Without the force of argument, the argument of force will prevail.

Learn that we cannot make free trade work for the poor unless we practice what we preach.

Learn that while we jealously guard our own police and judicial traditions, the criminals will run rings around us.

Fellow Liberals, we live in an age replete with political opportunity.

I believe the twenty-first century will be a Liberal century. Because ours is the message of the moment for humankind.

That's why Europe now has 5 Liberal Prime Ministers. Liberals are in government in 11 European states, including here in the Netherlands.

Liberals head the European Parliament and the European Commission. Liberals hold the balance of power in the European Parliament.

We are a growing family and a growing movement. Next year we stand to win twenty new seats in the expanded European Parliament. Maybe more.

We need to make this momentum work for us.

By making sure that the new rules on European political parties do not weaken the link between the party and the group in the European Parliament. In fact, by strengthening the links between group and party, and between national MPs and European MEPs.

By working to ensure the maximum number of Liberal Democrat Commissioners when the new Commission is appointed next year.

By making one of Europe's exceptional Liberal leaders our candidate for President of the Commission and campaigning to see them appointed.

And perhaps most of all, by being clear about why our message works, and how to make it work better.

Our Liberalism is a modern creed, but it has long traditions.

We draw on the Classical Liberalism of Locke and Rousseau and John Stuart Mill. We understand that the only measure of humanity is the individual. No society, no culture, no government, is sovereign over the mind or body of any one of us.

We understand the insights of Economic Liberalism. Of Adam Smith and David Riccardo. We believe that if you grant men and women the freedom to buy and sell at a free market then their hundred small enterprises will enrich our common enterprise. Smith called this 'our most sacred property...the property that every man has in his own labour'.

Yet we also know that Liberals who speak only of free individuals and free trade will never long enjoy success.

Because freedom means nothing without fraternity.

It is not enough to emancipate. We must also empower. If we cannot argue for solidarity and social justice then we do not deserve to be in power, and we never will be.

This part of our inheritance is the Social Liberalism of the great New Liberal tradition. Of Gladstone and Grundtvig and Karl-Herman Flach, who understood that in a democratic society, true freedom is not the absence of fetters, but the presence of fairness.

The twentieth century was the century in which war and intolerance and ethnic cleansing soaked our soil in blood. It was the century that added to our languages the words, 'totalitarian', 'genocide', and 'crime against humanity'.

This will be the century of Liberal democracy.

What will our words be?

Freedom. Tolerance. Democracy. Reform. Human Rights. These are words to transform our lives.

Words to free Europe's potential.

We can free the potential of Europe's people by making their political contract the envy of the world. By insisting on diversity. And celebrating it.

We can free the potential of Europe's political institutions by making them more open and democratic. By forcing a revolution in accountability at every level of European government so that people trust and respect the European Union.

*EU've got mail!*

We can free the potential of Europe's economy by unleashing the job-creating, prosperity-producing power of the world's largest single market. Europe needs a dynamic economy to prosper. We must cut away the red tape that hampers innovation and ties down Europe's entrepreneurs and small businesses. We must free people to buy and sell and move and work from Belfast to Budapest.

We can free the potential of Europe's sustainable technologies and lifestyles by making Europe the world leader in environmental enhancement. By committing to cleaner, safer forms of energy and embracing the world's highest standards of pollution control and renewable resource use.

We can free the potential of globalisation by making it work for everyone. We must insist on sustainable development and free and fair trade. We must open our own markets to the trade that can help the world's poorest escape the trap of poverty.

We can free the potential of Europe's global influence by speaking with a single voice. We must speak as one to give that voice credibility where it counts most.

That is why, Liberal Friends, our message for these elections is a simple but powerful one.

European Liberal Democrats.
Freeing Europe's Potential.

[1] *Sweden held a referendum on the euro on 14 September 2003. The No camp received 56.1% of the vote, to the Yes camp's 41.8%.*

[2] *The fifth World Trade Organisation ministerial was held in Cancun, Mexico at the beginning of September.*

[3] *19 Italians (12 of them Carabinieri) were killed in a bomb attack in Nasiriyah, Iraq on 12 November 2003. Nine Iraqis were also killed.*

*Appendix*

## IV. Speech to Parliament at conclusion of the Italian Presidency of the EU
*Letter of 22 December 2003*

Mr President, Liberals in this House expected rather more from the presidency of a country with a proud European tradition. In six short months, the presidency has conspired to undermine the Stability Pact, has shown contempt for the European Union's policy towards Russia and offended Canada.

The President-in-Office has treated us to a 40-minute catalogue of the achievements of his term of office. Yet it is hard to escape the conclusion that this presidency and IGC have been a personal failure for the President of the European Council. The 'piece of paper' in Mr Berlusconi's pocket turned out to be a gelato-stained napkin with a few bad jokes scribbled on it[1]. The President came to the IGC poorly prepared; he ignored the warnings of this House that holding back compromise proposals would produce this kind of stalemate.

While the Americans were digging Saddam Hussein out of a hole in Iraq to global acclaim, our leaders were digging themselves into a hole in Brussels.

A successful summit needed two things: political will on the part of the major countries, and skilful diplomatic leadership. It showed neither.

This IGC was not fated to fail - it chose to. Five countries walked away from an agreement which everybody needed but none of them wanted enough.

Yes, a delayed deal is better than a bad one. But the problem with postponing a decision by kicking it into the long grass is that you might not find it again. Especially with a crowded agenda ahead which includes negotiations on the next financial perspectives, talks on Turkish membership and elections in Spain, Britain and Italy.

So after a short post-mortem, the IGC must resume and must conclude its work under the Irish presidency. The Irish have Mr Ahern, one of Europe's most seasoned negotiators, and Mr Cox, the President of our own House, whose joy at the Charlemagne Prize[2] we share. It may be possible to relaunch the European Union. Our first Constitution deserves public debate and endorsement, and that requires a Treaty before the European elections in June 2004.

I would like to underline the extent of the concern felt by Liberal Democrats and Reformers in this House and beyond and our feeling that the actions of the larger Member States are plunging the European Union into a crisis which could endanger the democratic nature of our Union.

The summit conclusions are also a disappointment to us. There is nothing on Guantanamo Bay, despite the explicit demand of this House that our leaders should uphold the rights of the detainees. On Russia, the conclusions scandalously make no reference to elections which the OSCE called 'a regression in the democratisation process'.

The decision to bring the People's Republic of China into the Galileo programme seems to have encouraged talk of the lifting of the European embargo on selling arms to the world's only significant remaining Communist dictatorship.

On all these issues, the Council behaved as if it is ashamed of our values - or ignorant of them altogether.

At your press conference after the summit, President-in-Office, you said that but for the IGC, your presidency would be remembered as 'the most glorious of recent years'. Yet agreement on the five issues mentioned by the President of the Commission represents a meagre return on a presidency in which such high hopes were invested. If this was a glorious success, I would be fascinated to know your definition of a failure. You set your presidency the target of a Constitution by Christmas. By your own standards, you have failed.

[1] *Mr Berlusconi had mentioned that in his pocket was a piece of paper with a secret formula on it for solving the impasse over the voting system debate at the EU summit. He then told a joke about throwing someone out of a helicopter just days after a serious helicopter accident left Polish Prime Minister Leszek Miller in a full-body cast.*

*Appendix*

[2] *Pat Cox had recently been named to receive the Charlemagne prize for services to Europe, for his contribution to European integration in light of his work towards the historic enlargement of the EU. He shared the prize with Pope John Paul II.*

## Index

Ahern, Bertie ................................ 112, 120, 173
Air passenger data transfer ............. 56, 135-6, 141-2, 144, 147, 149-50, 151
Albright, Madeleine ...................... 23
Alibhai-Brown, Yasmin ................ 48
Andreasen, Marta ......................... 28, 35, 62
Annan, Kofi ................................. 124, 147
Ashdown, Paddy .......................... 70, 72
Ashrawi, Hanan ........................... 37
Asia .............................................. 11, 25, 33-4, 49-50, 57, 63-5, 88, 96, 99, 106, 111
Attwooll, Elspeth ......................... 58
Aznar, Jose Maria ........................ 17, 42, 49, 110
Barnard, Kay ................................ 132
Barnier, Michel ............................ 27, 62, 69, 146
Bayrou, Francois .......................... 136
Benedict, Douglas ........................ 28
Berlusconi, Silvio ......................... 66, 79-80, 81, 83, 98, 100, 101, 102, 111, 149, 173-4
Berzins, Andris ............................ 26
Beysen, Ward ............................... 24
Blair, Tony ................................... 42, 49, 51, 57, 60, 74, 110, 118, 149, 150, 159
Blix, Hans .................................... 53
Blood products directive .............. 152
Boateng, Paul ............................... 126
Bolkestein, Frits ........................... 153
Boogerd-Quaak, Johanna ............. 141, 144
Bowles, Sharon ............................ 101
Breed, Colin ................................. 151
Britain & Europe ......................... 11, 57, 60, 67, 70-1, 74, 100, 118, 119, 123, 149, 150
Brown, Gordon ............................ 450, 74
Bush, George ............................... 17, 26, 53, 91, 129, 160
Caveri, Luciano ............................ 27
Chichester, Giles .......................... 84
Chirac, Jacques ............................ 47, 54, 58, 83, 110, 160, 164
Clarke, Chris ................................ 99
Clegg, Nick .................................. 16, 72, 100

*Index*

Common Agricultural Policy ........16, 51, 74, 78, 151, 156
Cotter, Brian ...................................121
Cox, Pat ..........................................10, 39, 96, 120, 138, 143, 150, 166, 173, 175
Crespo, Enrique Baron ..................111
Danish Presidency .........................32, 39-40
Davies, Chris .................................35
Davis, Ann .....................................12
de Clercq, Willy.............................92
de Vries, Gijs .................................141
Defence policy...............................38-9, 59, 83, 95, 99
Diamantopoulou, Anna..................101, 146
Disability .......................................88
Drnovsek, Janez.............................31
Duff, Andrew ................................13, 67
Duncan Smith, Ian.........................14
ELDR seminars .............................48, 127, 135, 136, 143
ELDR.............................................5, 15, 24, 25, 54, 61, 76, 77, 84, 94, 95, 96, 98, 101, 103, 109-10, 120, 125, 128, 132, 143, 150, 165-172
Enlargement...................................11, 13, 15, 20, 22, 30-1, 32, 35, 36, 40, 47, 60-1, 65, 86, 99, 117, 124, 131, 145, 147, 156-7, 158-9, 166
Environment/Health ......................16, 22, 35, 41, 65-6, 67, 135, 139-40, 148, 153, 165-6
Erdogan, Recep Tayyip..................36, 69
EU budget......................................97, 122, 127
EU Constitution.............................13, 17, 20, 28, 47, 50, 67, 70-1, 82, 85, 104, 117, 131, 142, 149, 162, 166
EU Economy ................................13, 54-5, 58, 104, 105, 117, 118, 122, 154-5, 159, 166
Euro ...............................................11, 86, 87, 104-5, 159-60
European Commission ..................17, 28, 32, 35, 75-6, 81-2, 83-4, 90, 118, 141-2, 146
Evans, Judy....................................137
Farage, Nigel .................................12
Fischler, Franz ..............................17, 32, 51, 74
Fisheries.........................................18, 32, 58, 70, 121
Fogh Rasmussen, Anders...............32, 40
Ford, Glyn .....................................128
Frasnyiuk, Wladislaw ...................37

Fullick, Lawrence ..........................133
Geremek, Bronislaw ......................37
Gibraltar..........................................84, 124
Gillard, Karen .................................137
Giscard d'Estaing, Valéry ...............10, 52, 75, 85
Greek Presidency............................42, 48, 54
Guantanamo Bay ............................100, 122-3, 137
Hain, Peter ......................................28, 67
Hall, Rachel....................................88
Hanney, Malcolm ...........................77
Heathcoat-Amory, David................67
Holloway, Shirley ..........................12
Hoyer, Werner.................................5
Hughes, Simon ...............................55
Human Rights.................................84, 105-6, 122-3, 124, 126, 161
Immigration ....................................20, 34, 41-2, 72-3, 124
International Criminal Court..........16, 22, 29
Iraq..................................................24, 26, 47, 52-3, 54, 83, 161
Irish Presidency ..............................107, 120, 131, 133, 137, 142, 173
Italian Presidency ...........................66-7, 79-80, 100-101, 102, 111, 173-5
Jackson, Caroline ...........................125, 128
Jenkins, Roy ...................................102, 128
Jewellry hallmarking .....................93-4
Johnston, Lord Russell ...................30
Kallas, Siim ....................................125, 153
Kennedy, Charles............................14, 29, 30, 150
Kent, Sarah .....................................28
Khodorkovsky, Mikhail .................108
Kindermann, Heinz ........................128
Kinnock, Glenys.............................106
Kinnock, Neil .................................17, 28, 36, 76, 81
Kyprianou, Marcos .........................159
Laws, David....................................123
Lee, Christine .................................27
Lee, Martin .....................................57
Lindh, Anna....................................86
Ludford, Baroness (Sarah) .............123
Lynne, Liz.......................................85
Maaten, Jules..................................24
Maclennan of Rogart, Lord .............20, 67
Main, James....................................137

*Index*

Manders, Toine ..............................65
Media pluralism............................26, 29, 149
MEPs statute..................................38, 71, 73-4, 78-9, 112, 125
Middle East ...................................37, 108, 143-4
Morillon, Philippe ........................59
Mulder, Jan....................................16, 97, 139
Nicholson of Winterbourne,
Baroness (Emma).........................126, 138
Nieslon, Poul ................................106
Parish, Neil ...................................136
Parker, George ..............................38
Patten, Chris .................................106
Poettering, Hans Gert ...................111, 120
Potocnik, Janez.............................125, 153
Prodi, Romano..............................17, 32, 79, 84, 87, 89, 102, 120, 136, 153, 154
Rainsy, Sam ..................................88
Regional policy.............................28, 62, 68-9, 92-3, 155
Roche, Dick ..................................133
Ruane, John ..................................27
Rusko, Pavel .................................27
Russia ............................................99, 108, 133
Sanders, Adrian ............................32
Sanders, Marieke..........................24, 124
Schreyer, Michaele .......................36, 76
Schulz, Martin ..............................80
Senegal ..........................................96-7
Shadrick, Des ...............................28
Shui-bien, Chien...........................33, 49
Simitis, Costas...............................36, 42
Smidt, Steffan................................17
Solbes, Pedro ................................76, 81, 83-4, 87, 90, 118, 146
Soon Juan, Chee ...........................36
Sorensen, Ole ................................62
Spanish Presidency.......................17, 42
Steel, David ..................................6, 132
Stem cell research ........................103, 107
Stevens, John & Sheila..................133
Stockton, Lord...............................67
Stolojan, Theodor .........................99
Stuart, Gisela ................................67

Suu Kyi, Aung San ........................34
Telicka, Pavel................................153
Terrorism... .....................................12,27,117,138-9,141
Teverson, Robin ............................62
Thomas of Wallisdown,
Baroness ........................................55
Titley, Gary ....................................119
Transatlantic relations ...................23, 90-2, 135, 160
Transport policy ............................24, 49, 81, 96, 98, 102
Treleaven, Mike .............................35, 133
Tyler, Paul ......................................151
Uribe, Alvaro .................................127-8
van den Bos, Bob ..........................84
Verheugen, Gunther .......................145, 157
Verhofstadt, Guy ............................96
Wade, Abdoulaye ...........................89-7
Welch, Tony ...................................77, 99
Yavlinksi, Grigory ........................108
Younger-Ross, Richard .................121

# Information/Addresses

**Presidencies of the European Union 1998-2006:**
1998 United Kingdom, Austria
1999 Germany, Finland
2000 Portugal, France
2001 Sweden, Belgium
2002 Spain, Denmark
2003 Greece, Italy
2004 Ireland, Netherlands
2005 Luxembourg, United Kingdom
2006 Austria, Finland

*************************************************

**Graham Watson MEP:** www.grahamwatsonmep.org

| *Constituency office:* | *Brussels office:* |
|---|---|
| Bagehot's Foundry | European Parliament |
| Beard's Yard | Rue Wiertz |
| Langport | B-1047 Brussels |
| Somerset TA10 9PS | Belgium |
| UK | |
| euro_office@cix.co.uk | gwatson@europarl.eu.int |

**Liberal Democrats**: www.libdems.org.uk

**ELDR party**: www.eldr.org

**ELDR Group in the European Parliament**: www.eurolib.org

**European Parliament**: www.europarl.eu.int

**European Union**: www.europa.eu.int